*The Homemaker's Book of
Time & Money Savers*

The Homemaker's Book of

TIME &
MONEY SAVERS

Jean Laird

THE STEPHEN GREENE PRESS

Brattleboro, Vermont

This book has been produced in the United States of America
It is published by The Stephen Greene Press, Brattleboro, Vermont
05301.

LIBRARY OF CONGRESS CATALOGING IN PUBLICATION DATA

Laird, Jean E
  The homemaker's Book of time & money savers.

  1. Consumer education. 2. Home economics. I. Title.
II. Title: Book of time & money savers. III. Title:
Time & money savers.
TX335.L28   640.73   79-11496
ISBN 0-8289-0345-X
ISBN 0-8289-0346-8 pbk.

Contents

Preface

MY SINCEREST thanks to my family and friends, and to the readers of "Time & Money Savers," my column in *Lady's Circle* magazine, for their many helpful suggestions and novel ideas for stretching the budget. Without them *The Homemaker's Book of Time & Money Savers* could not have been written.

What you will find in this book are lots of hints and tricks designed to help the manager of your household, not necessarily to spend less, but to get more for his or her money, so that your family's income will go farther. Each chapter contains enough budget-cutting tricks to save you the price of the book. Read it, use it, enjoy it. I sincerely hope it will help you to stretch your budget to yield some extra cash for the things you enjoy in life.

Jean E. Laird

·*Introduction*·

WE ARE TOLD that half of the couples who come to family service agencies for counseling report severe problems with the handling of money, making it one of the major emotional battlegrounds of marriage today. Often, it is not the lack of money that causes the trouble, but the misuse of it!.

Today's homemaker realizes that she can read volumes of books on keeping a budget, but they are not the answer. True, it helps to set up a certain number of dollars to be spent on food, clothing, recreation, and necessary living expenses. However, it is the *things you actually buy* with your dollars that make the difference between enjoying your funds to the fullest or finding them miserably inadequate.

Grocery Shopping

Are women better grocery shoppers than men? Surveys show that many men are prone to go hog-wild in the supermarket. You can send them out to buy staples for the weekend and they will come back loaded down with anchovies, wild rice, and jumbo-size cans of whatever else has caught their fancy on the gourmet shelf. And they don't seem to feel the least bit guilty about the pickled snails and sardines in mustard sauce that were pitched after one bite. Why? Because they usually don't have to account for the food budget.

Recently, shoppers in Yonkers, New York, participated in a program designed to help them get the most value for their money in the consumer market. They discovered the following astounding facts about buying:

- Used car prices at some local lots included a charge of 42 percent on installment payments!
- Charting day-to-day prices on frozen orange juice, for example, they found an 18- to 20-cent difference between two stores for the identical brand and size of can.
- Supermarkets tended to raise prices about two weeks in advance of a holiday, then dropped them back to stimulate sales.
- In analyzing advertising claims, it was almost impossible to distinguish facts from glittering generalities such as "twice as much," "works faster," or "secret ingredient."
- One pays dearly for the convenience of ready-to-eat meals.

Our buying habits are part of our total living style. Realizing this fact might not change our shopping habits much, but it can give us something to think about the next time we are trapped in a long line at the checkout counter.

Money Saver's Test

Here is a little test to see how you and your mate rate on money matters and thriftiness. Be honest, and the results may help you to spend your money more wisely, getting the very most for each dollar:

1. Do you save money through a payroll savings plan, credit union, or bank?

A. Regularly
B. Occasionally
C. Never

2. When grocery shopping, do you and your mate buy:
   A. The basic foods on your list only
   B. Basic foods plus a few treats
   C. More gourmet foods and treats than necessities

3. When planning for dinner guests, do you and your mate:
   A. Try to stay within the regular budget you have set up
   B. Splurge just a little
   C. Forget the budget and consider the occasion reason for extravagance

4. In the initial burst of enthusiasm over a new hobby, do either of you:
   A. Search the want-ads and buy used equipment
   B. Purchase beginner's new equipment
   C. Buy expensive professional equipment

5. Do you buy gifts for each other:
   A. Only on birthdays and holidays
   B. On birthdays, holidays, and as an occasional surprise
   C. Every time one of you expresses a desire for something

6. When you take a holiday, yearly vacation, or even a weekend trip to visit your mother, do you both prefer travel accommodations that are:
   A. Economy
   B. Economy with a few frills
   C. First class no matter how many "holidays" you have had that year

7. When dining out with other people, do you usually order:
   A. The least expensive meal
   B. A moderately priced meal
   C. The most expensive meal

8. When purchasing your household furniture or an appliance, do you and your mate insist upon:
   A. The most economical model

B. A model with a few "extras"

C. The most expensive model

9. When buying a new car, do you insist upon:

   A. A stripped-down model in the economy price bracket

   B. A model in the middle price bracket with the most "extras"

   C. The most expensive automobile available

10. When renting an apartment or buying your first home, did you:

    A. House-hunt until you were sure you had acquired the least expensive residence providing the necessary number of rooms

    B. Settle for spending a few extra dollars for the luxury of having a nearby pool or a neighborhood inhabited by couples in your own age group

    C. Insist upon the most expensive and luxurious home, even though it took a tremendous bite into your budget

11. Have you agreed to provide separate and appropriate personal allowances for you and your husband?

    A. Definite setup with no allowance for deviation

    B. Half of the time

    C. Never—each takes whatever he or she wants to spend personally

12. Do you operate from a planned budget, looking at all expenses for a year at a time?

    A. Always

    B. We try, but don't always stick to it

    C. Never—we know soon enough how it is going to come out in the end

13. Do you try to pay off debts as soon as possible, regardless of the agreed amount of payment?

    A. Always pay more than necessary

    B. Sometimes pay more than is required

    C. Never—if we agree to pay it off in a year, we are content to let it take that long

14. Do you carry an appropriate amount of insurance, in terms of your present needs as well as probable future needs?

    A. Yes—we have it reviewed periodically to be sure it is adequate

    B. We think we have enough coverage

    C. We carry a minimum, hoping nothing major will assail us

15. Before making major purchases do you study the publications of consumers' organizations, consult advertising in the local newspapers, review government bulletins, etc., in order to buy wisely?

    A. Always—personal desire often takes the back seat to consumer reports

    B. Sometimes—if the reports are handy and the ads are featuring the wanted item that week

    C. Never—we go by instinct and personal desire alone when we buy the things we are going to live with for awhile

16. Do you pay cash rather than buying on the installment plan, except in very special cases?

    A. Always—we wait until we have the money in hand before making a purchase

    B. Most of the time, unless the item in question represents a major monetary outlay—such as a car, house, etc.

    C. Never—why pay cash when you can enjoy something while you are paying for it?

17. Do you consider the biggest cost of owning a car the depreciation (or replacement)—not just the gas, oil, and necessary repairs?

    A. Always—riding the buses and subways is a small price to pay for transportation. An automobile can nickel-and-dime you to death

    B. This is an important consideration, but sometimes the joy of having your own transportation offsets the cost if it is a luxury you can afford

    C. Never—no matter how you do it, you have to pay to get around and, after all, everything depreciates, doesn't it?

18. At income tax time, do you read up on all the latest tax requirements so you can be fully informed and take advantage of any savings to which you are entitled?

    A. Always—both husband and wife spend the month before the tax deadline going through all possible publications carrying articles regarding possible deductions ·

    B. No—if things appear too complicated for us in any given year, we pay an income tax expert to do the job for us

    C. Never—in fact, we usually fill out the "short form," trusting the government to recognize our particular situation and give back any funds we might have coming

19. Do you keep enough cash in a savings plan to carry you, if necessary, for at least six months on a reduced living scale?

    A. Certainly—we wouldn't sleep nights if we didn't have at least six month's salary set aside

    B. I think we could squeak by for a half year if we absolutely had to—definitely "tightening the belt"

    C. We have trouble making our funds stretch from month to month

20. Do you ever keep financial secrets from each other?

    A. Never—we often feel guilty about "surprising" each other with minor gifts

    B. Sometimes—when we know it isn't of earth-shattering importance

    C. Always—let him worry about the things he buys, and I will worry when I have spread my funds too thinly

Scoring: If you have checked (A) every time, you are so economical that you probably argue just as much about money as the naive couple who has never learned to manage a dime. If you have checked (A) even ten times, you are still pretty economical. If the majority of your answers were (B), you will probably get along very well in this monetary world of ours. Those of you who have checked (C) in the majority of instances are heading toward financial disaster.

Read on. Here are some dandy ideas for stretching your dollars. Homemakers all over the country have found them to be successful, and so will you!

·1·

Shopping Tricks

MOST AMERICANS live on fixed incomes, at least in the short run. Just so many dollars are forthcoming each week. If you can keep within your limits, you can live with ease and grace. Sometimes it is the *way* you spend your money that makes the difference.

Every homemaker tries to achieve the best possible results for herself and her family with the money she has to spend. However, we must admit that in this affluent society of ours, shopping is a constant struggle with temptation— especially if there are several credit cards trying to burn a hole in milady's pocketbook.

The "thrifty" shopper does not necessarily master the art of buying less, but she has learned to *waste* less, stretching her funds to cover luxuries in addition to the necessities.

Thrifty shopping can be fun as well as profitable, and it can fill a real basic need for creativity. Most of us don't go in for soap-making, rug-weaving, canning, and preserving like the homemakers of yesteryear. Even if we do pursue some of these activities, we know they aren't absolutely essential to the family's well-being, as they once were. But thrifty shopping today *is*. A lot of satisfaction can be derived by the homemaker when she makes an honest effort to become the best purchasing agent any family ever had.

Supermarket Tips

Learning to shop wisely is a big job. Did you know that the average supermarket deals with from 12,000 to 20,000 different items? Joe D. tells us about the time his wife sent him to the supermarket to buy a box of laundry soap. "Any kind will do," she told him. "Just so I can get this laundry done today."

Upon Joe's return, he informed her that there were 69 different brands and sizes to choose from, each staring at him with bright-colored labels and promises of "brighter brights and whiter whites." He said, "They were not only marked—'Large,' 'Super,' 'King Size,' 'Family Size,' 'Regular,' and 'Giant'—but they came in 33, 47½, 55, 82, 110, and 250 pound sizes. Some were packed loosely (I picked them up and shook them), and some were packed tight. Some had kitchen towels inserted into the box as an added bonus, some had glassware, and still others had pieces of silver or bath towels."

Joe continued, "As fate would have it, my eye caught a bright-colored red and yellow label on a familiar-sounding brand that read '10 cents off.' Always one to be on the thrifty side, I selected the discount brand and trotted off, happy and proud that I had taken advantage of a bargain and had done my share to shave a few cents off our already staggering grocery bill.

"While driving home, I began to wonder: '10 *cents off what?*' Was it off the regular retail price which varies from store to store? Was it off yesterday's price—or last week's going rate? What was the regular 'retail' price anyway? I had no idea. The price stamped on the box top was 98 cents, and I had paid 98 cents for it. Had the grocer stamped the box *after* he had subtracted the 10 cents or was the sale price 98 cents less the 10 cents? If so, I hadn't saved a cent. I decided to stop thinking about it after I almost took the back end off a lady crossing the street with a shopping cart loaded with groceries.

"My wife laughed when I told her I felt the supermarkets displayed their wares like well-laid out mine fields, hoping the customers will fall victim. She was quick to inform me that even if I had ended up with the lowest priced detergent, ounce for ounce, it wouldn't mean that I had come home with the greatest bargain. It seems some detergents stretch twice as far because the housewife has to use only half as much per load. At this point, I gladly admitted defeat. I trust all future shopping to her . . . and hope that she is thrifty."

As food costs tend to skyrocket, we oftentimes feel it is virtually impossible to adequately compare packaging and pricing without a master's degree in math. If we can uncover some of the reasons behind this consumer confusion, we will succeed in unscrambling the supermarket puzzle and end up on the "thrifty" side of the food budget.

Bargain-hunting is as natural to women as breathing. Yet, a recent Michigan study of housewives with a college background showed that 43 percent were unable to pick out the best buys in supermarket items. Official figures show the average U.S. family spends slightly more than $1500 annually on food. Yet, Senate investigators estimate that 15 percent of this total amount is "lost dollar value" due to the confusion of the purchaser.

Packaging and Buyer Psychology

We do not want to imply that manufacturers are using deceptive *packaging* and trying to fool us. However, the wise shopper is alert and makes her purchases with awareness. For instance, in many cases "air space" in packaging is very necessary to insure that the contents remains fresh until opened. For this reason, "air space" is legal even if only 65 percent of the usable space contains the actual product. It is up to the purchaser to decide how much air space he is willing to pay for.

Here is another example of how packaging can work: We have all seen a 7-inch candy bar selling for 10 or 15 cents, containing a cardboard insert which is 7 inches long. A 5-inch candy bar is placed strategically in the center of this cardboard. Who buys these candy bars? Candy-lovers of all ages. Obviously, the length of the candy bar is important to the purchaser and the difference between the inside and outside length is deceiving. However, the cardboard insert is necessary to protect the candy from being crushed during shipment, as well as on the display stand, where it may even be stood on end. The alert shopper keeps the actual size of the candy bar in mind when he makes his choice.

The way stores price their *sales* is another example of how they use buyer psychology. Stores learned long ago that $4.98 *sounds* closer to $4 than it does to $5. And, even though you and I know perfectly well what the score is, we sometimes respond emotionally to the "value" signal in the odd-cents price. During sales, stores often carry this device even further. Instead of the familiar 98 or 69 cents ending to prices, they may pick a less usual sum, such as 87 or 74 cents, to put over the idea that special savings are being offered.

A recent survey conducted by the advertising industry showed that less than 20 percent of the supermarket patrons today actually take the time necessary to shop intelligently. Most decisions are made *after* the customer enters the store, because she doesn't carry a shopping list with her—nor has she planned the menu for the week. This fact accounts for the colorful and inviting displays found in most supermarkets.

The wise shopper is not confused or misled by island *displays* or end-of-the-aisle stocked displays. She knows that if these items are not featured in the newspaper ads or on the window posters, chances are they are the regular off-the-shelf price. She is alert and sharp-witted. She knows how to take advantage of food specials and to recognize when a bargain is a bargain. This is the way she gets the most from her food dollar.

The "secret" of thrifty consumer purchasing is *aware-*

ness. Knowing about the lack of standardization in packaging laws, contents, and price, the wise shopper is alert to ways to recover some of the dollars that are lost. For instance, she realizes that in many instances, the product ingredients are listed on the *label* in the order of content (the first item being the highest percentage of the product, the second item the second highest, etc.). A can of beef stew may list the contents as "potatoes, carrots, and beef." Obviously, there are more potatoes and carrots than beef. Considering that the average homemaker's recipe for beef stew would be at least 40 percent beef, this is not the greatest buy. A thrifty buyer would buy potatoes and carrots, or mixed vegetables, and add the stew meat at home, saving up to 50 percent on a serving for four.

She also knows that the *family-size pack* of any grocery product is not always the most economical. It takes but a few minutes to figure out the cost per ounce, and this savings can amount to dollars in your pocket. There are times when it is less expensive to buy two packages of a smaller size, and they are often more convenient to store than one large box.

Substitution is another way many homemakers elasticize their food budget. You may never have thought of using a substitute such as dry milk, but it will be worth your while to at least experiment with it. The New York University School of Home Economics recently conducted a class for homemakers and showed that in mixtures such as puddings and batters, dry milk is almost impossible to distinguish from fresh milk. If you can replace one quart of milk a day with the dry product, the NYU experts estimate that you will save about $1.26 a week, or over $60 a year! Further, imitation milk products manufactured from either fresh skim milk or reconstituted nonfat dry milk have been proven nutritionally comparable to whole milk products.

Fruit drinks are one of the most puzzling items on the market today. Even the can sizes give no indication of true value, because the major component may be plain water. According to Federal standards, a "fruit juice" can contain only juice and no water. Yet, "nectar" may contain some water. "Ade," "punch," and "drink" may consist of sugar, water, and imitation flavoring—or they may have a low percentage of actual juice mixed with low-cost additives. "Imitation" or "flavored" drinks usually contains no natural juices, but consist of artificial flavors and citrus oils.

What about *cereals?* They can produce another shopper's dilemma. We found in one supermarket a 10-ounce box of cereal at 35 cents. Right next to it on the same shelf is a competitive brand of equal quality and content selling at 37 cents for 13 ounces. Both boxes are the same height and width, but the 13-ouncer is a half inch thicker, so obviously it is the better buy. We also notice that "convenience packaging," such as eight of the 1-ounce boxes of cereal usually sold as "individual servings," can cost up to *twice* as much per ounce as a larger size. And, did you know that a bowl of oatmeal has many times more natural vitamins than some of the packaged cereals which far exceed oatmeal in price?

The wise shopper also knows that the true value of any product is its *cost per ounce* compared to its quality. What does this mean? Pick up a can of pears marked "Serves 4 to 6." Perhaps in your estimation it will barely serve a family of three. Remember, there is no industry standard for the word "serving." What might fill one husband's stomach, might be only a light snack for another.

Supermarket Survival

Here are a few hints for thrifty grocery shopping:

Write your *grocery list* on the back of an empty envelope and slip the coupons you plan to redeem into it. This will keep everything together in your handbag, and you won't forget to turn these little money savers in at the checkout counter.

The housewife who really wants to save money on her food budget always makes out her *menus* for at least one full week at a time. Why? Because it is much easier to visualize leftover possibilities on paper. She also checks the ads in the newspapers and takes advantage of "specials," taking into careful consideration the distance of the stores from her home and the cost of gasoline. She checks the recipes she will be using to be sure all the ingredients she needs are on hand or on the list of things to be purchased that week. This will save her extra, costly, time-consuming trips to the store as well as money that might be spent buying duplicates of things she is not sure about.

It costs more to put a product into a box than a *bag*, and these higher costs are usually passed on to the consumer as higher prices. *Chain Store Age*, a magazine of the retailing industry, says that supermarket items you can buy in bags—like flour, sugar, and rice—are about 18 percent cheaper than the same items in boxes.

Keep a *portable cooler* in the car during the summer months and use it to keep meat and other refrigerated items, as well as frozen foods, from spoiling while driving home from the supermarket.

Keep your eyes open for advertisements of dealer specials, and carry a copy of the ad when shopping. The stock clerk may not always have time to mark down every item in stock, and the checkout clerk may not be aware of every day's specials.

Before purchasing the item with the biggest price *discount*, first take into consideration whether the price may have been set too high in the first place. When quantity specials are run, such as five for $1 or four for 89 cents, take advantage or the group-price bargain whenever you can.

When buying "all beef" or "all meat" *processed*

meats," check the actual content. "All beef" or "all meat" products could contain less actual meat than those offered with added cereal. The fat content of the product is the deciding factor, and it should be clearly marked on the package.

When buying *cheeses,* check the "moisture content." We have found some to be more water than cheese! One widely advertised brand contains 58 percent moisture, another 52 percent, and still another only 47 percent.

When buying canned *chicken soup,* check to see that at least 2 percent of the content is chicken. If the main ingredients are additives and water, it would be more economical to buy a base broth and add the meat at home.

When buying *frozen breaded items* such as shrimp, check to see how much shrimp you are getting. By regulation, such products need only contain 50 percent shrimp or meat. These are "convenience" products and the breading can make up the other 50 percent.

Choose *peanut butter* by the actual peanut content and cost per ounce. We found that one leading peanut butter manufacturer offers two products—one with 72 percent peanuts and the other with 90 percent peanut content—both at the same price per ounce!

At the *checkout counter,* control the feeding of the purchases to the clerk. There will be much less chance for error in ringing up the proper amount.

Managing Your Cash and Credit Cards

Many of us have *credit cards* from many different establishments. Add the phone numbers of these stores to your personal directory, along with the number on the charge plate. This will not only save you time in searching through your credit cards when you order merchandise by telephone, but it will provide you with an additional listing of credit card numbers, should your cards be lost or stolen.

At one time or another, practically everyone has reached into her pocket or purse for money, only to discover it is gone! Studies show that last year, 7 million Americans had a similar experience. In most cases, the money was lost, stolen, or destroyed through carelessness, usually in fairly small amounts.

What kind of people *lose their money* carelessly? According to a recent survey compiled by two research organizations for the American Express Company:

- Nearly twice as many women as men lose cash (one women in 12, compared to one man in 20).
- College-educated adults are more loss prone than high-school graduates.
- Individuals in managerial positions lose money more frequently than skilled workers, farmers, and people in professions.
- Youths in the 18- to 20-year age bracket lose money more frequently than any other age group. One in 9 loses cash every year, while for people over 60, the loss frequency is one person in 25.
- Level of income makes little difference in being prone to loss. Rich and poor lose money with almost equal frequency.

In addition, the report notes that most people remember *where* they lost cash, but not *how* it disappeared. In most cases, cash losses can be avoided or minimized if these rules are observed:

- Carry as little cash as possible.
- Keep money in a secure place in your wallet or purse.
- Keep large sums in a bank or other financial institution.

- Know how much money you have with you when you leave the confines of your home.
- When traveling, use money orders, travelers checks, or credit cards.
- Do not leave your purse lying on a store counter, or on a seat in a waiting room, rest room, or restaurant.

Take care of your hard-earned cash, learn to spend it wisely, and make it work for you to provide the things you want most in life. After all, you earned it—and you have a right to enjoy it. Budgeting is *not* penny-pinching, but learning to spend wisely so your money will stretch . . . and stretch . . . and stretch!

·2·

Your Food Budget—
How To Beat It

NEARLY ALL OF our meals are built around meats and meat alternates, so it makes good sense—and cents—to learn to buy meats wisely. Have are some tips from food economists and the Agricultural Research Service that will help to make *your* food dollars go a bit further.

Hints on Meat

The price per pound for meat is not the most reliable guide to the best buys. Why? It is the number of *servings* you can get per pound that counts, and this varies with the "cut" you buy, as well as the amount of fat, bone, and gristle.

For example, lamb chops that sell for $1.04 per pound actually cost 46 cents per 3-ounce serving of cooked lean meat. In comparison, boneless rump roast at $1.19 per pound costs 40 cents per serving. Although the rump roast costs more per pound, it is a better buy because you get more servings per pound from it.

The discriminating shopper also knows that a pound of

ground round at 89 cents a pound may be a much better buy than ground beef at 69 cents, because the latter contains a high percentage of fat that is lost in cooking.

The lower *grades* of beef, USDA Good and USDA Standard, provide more lean meat and generally cost less than USDA Prime and USDA Choice. The lower grades are less tender and juicy than the two top grades, but prepared properly they are tasty and satisfying.

How do you determine the size of the *turkey or chicken* you will need for a meal? A small turkey (less than 12 pounds) will yield one serving per pound. Bigger birds yield more—a 16-pound turkey will give you 20 to 28 servings. Frankly, the big bird is your best buy, even if you freeze half for a later date. Moreover, the initial work of stuffing, etc., is the same as for the smaller bird.

Chickens sold whole generally cost a few cents less per pound than chickens cut up, and considerably less than chicken pieces such as breasts and thighs or legs.

Each year, *cold cuts* are becoming more popular fare for use in sandwiches and at lunch or suppertime. Did you know there are 200 varieties of sausages and luncheon meats to choose from, differing mostly in the way they are cooked, prepared, or seasoned? The most common varieties are sausages and luncheon meats.

Sausages are made by grinding or chopping pork, beef, or veal, seasoning with spices, and stuffing the mixture into casings which give them shape. The varieties of sausage used as cold cuts are usually cooked, smoked and cooked, or are dried and cured. (For instance, a *salami* is an air-dried sausage which may or may not have been smoked.) They consist basically of pork and beef trimmings and are highly seasoned. *Hard* or *German salami* is compact and dry, differing from the softer *Italian salami* in the way it is seasoned. *Cervelat* is a semi-dry sausage product that has been smoked. It is made of pork and/or beef, and is seasoned with garlic. *Bologna* consists of pork and/or beef seasoned with pepper, cloves, coriander, and ginger. It is much softer than salami and is usually larger in diameter, giving bigger slices. *Liver sausage* and *liverwurst* are made of finely ground and cured pork and liver, seasoned with salt and pepper, onions, marjoram, and sometimes mustard, cloves, ginger, and mace. A similar product is called *Braunschweiger.*

Luncheon meats are specially prepared meat products which have been pressed or cooked in oblong pans to retain a loaf shape. They are sometimes dipped in a gelatin solution. Prepared from both cured and uncured meats, they are rarely smoked and can be found in sliced packaged form. *Honey loaf* is a meat mixture similar to bologna, usually made with pork. It is flavored with spices, honey, and sometimes pimentos and pickles. *Peppered loaf* is usually made from lean coarse pieces of beef which have been cured. This loaf is covered with cracked, black peppercorns. *Olive loaf* is a blend of lean beef and pork, finely chopped and seasoned, and mixed with whole stuffed olives. *Macaroni and cheese loaf* contains finely ground beef and pork, along with sharp cheese and macaroni. *Spiced luncheon meat* consists of pieces of cured pork and/or beef pressed together and highly seasoned. *Headcheese* is a mixture of hogs-head meat and pork products, cured and stuffed into casings or pressed into shape. *Pickle and pimento loaf* is finely chopped lean pork and beef to which sweet pickles and pimentos have been added. *Souse* is similar to headcheese except for the addition of a vinegar pickle which gives souse a sweet–sour flavor. *Jellied tongue* is either pork, beef, or veal tongue which is cured and cooked. It is placed in casings or loaf pans, and gelatin is added to give it a molded shape when cooled. *Pressed chicken and turkey* loaves are pieces of chicken and turkey, mildly seasoned, cooked, and pressed into shape.

Have trouble slicing around the bone of a *ham* without a lot of waste? Ask the butcher to cut the ham for you *lengthwise* (right through the flat side—even if he has never heard of it before). Cut it into two pieces, the way you would cut a hot dog bun in half. After you cut the ham the bone will fall right out, leaving the meat ready for slicing!

Keeping Food Items Fresh and Tasty

If *olive oil* is stored in a warm room, it gets rancid in a very short while. Keep it covered tightly in the refrigerator. The cold will harden the olive oil, but it will quickly melt when it is placed at room temperature for a few minutes.

When a jar of *honey* becomes crystallized or *syrups* turn a bit sugary, they can easily be liquified by placing the container in a pan of hot water.

Do you sometimes have *glass bottles* which have been stored on your refrigerator door come crashing out, wasting the contents? Put all dressings, syrups, sauces, etc., in empty plastic bottles. They can be marked according to contents with freezer marking pencil. These markings can easily be removed with kitchen cleanser, making the plastic bottle available for a different food. No more breakage, should the children happen to knock a bottle out onto the floor.

When heat has turned that *baking chocolate* in your cupboard white, there is no need to throw it out. When the chocolate is melted for cooking purposes, it will turn brown again, and there is usually no loss of flavor.

When *cream* won't whip, try adding the white of an egg. Chill thoroughly, then whip.

If you store your *eggs* in the egg compartment attached to your refrigerator door, chances are you don't save the egg cartons. What is more annoying than setting your eggs on the countertop whenever you are about to use them, only to find they have rolled off and broken? Why not use one of those little plastic berry boxes to hold your eggs on the countertop? All danger of breakage will be eliminated.

Ever find that you just don't have an orange or lemon on hand, and need only a little bit of *grated rind* for a recipe? The next time you store your lemons and oranges in the refrigerator, wash them and grate off some of the skins. You can then measure these grated pieces, place a teaspoon in a small square of plastic wrap, fold securely, and place these small packets into a plastic container in your freezer. You will never again be without grated orange or lemon rind for your cake batters and icings.

When making *lemon twists*, instead of refrigerating a partially used lemon, remove all the lemon peel at once. Freeze the twists in a small container. Extract the juice from the lemon and freeze it in an ice cube tray. You can then pop the frozen lemon cubes into a plastic bag or container and place them in the freezer.

When doing your grocery shopping, do you oftentimes put the *bags of groceries* on the front seat beside you? You won't have to worry about sudden stops if you fasten the extra set of seat belts around the bags.

You can also put a deep, strong carton between the front and back seats of your car. Put the bags into this carton, making it impossible for the bags to fall over. (Have you noticed it is always the bag containing the eggs that makes the crash landing on the way home?)

Or, if you own a station wagon or van, place an instant-mounting spring tension curtain rod across the back of the wagon to make a pen to hold your packages.

When covering a *meringue pie* with transparent wrap, lightly grease the wrap with cooking oil before covering the pie. It will come off easily without disturbing the meringue.

After a can of *chocolate syrup* has been opened and refrigerated, it becomes difficult to pour. Why not take a thoroughly washed plastic squeeze bottle (the kind that contains pancake syrup), and empty the chocolate syrup into it as soon as the can is opened? The top closes to keep the syrup fresh, and all you have to do is squeeze the bottle to pour the syrup.

If you take advantage of an *ice cream* sale to buy for future use, overwrap the ice cream cartons with freezer paper so they don't dry out before you get to using them.

When your family doesn't drink all the pop in those *flip-topped cans*, take a piece of cellophane tape and put it across the opening. Return the can to the refrigerator and the carbonation will stay in for some time.

If your *salt* gets damp and lumps in the shaker, turn a jelly glass over the shaker—and you will have no more caked salt.

Have you ever overcooked the *mashed potatoes* so they became soggy when you added the milk? Next time, sprinkle them with powdered milk, for the fluffiest mashed potatoes ever.

Are you usually stuck with half-empty boxes of *cereal* that go stale before they are consumed? Start saving those glass jars that instant coffee comes in, and use them to store the leftover cereals. It is easy to see what is in them, and they can be decorated with a few decals to give the illusion of a canister set.

Oftentimes a recipe calls for just a few drops of *lemon juice*. Don't slice that lemon, as it will probably dry out before you have had a chance to use it again. Stick a sharp wooden toothpick into the lemon and then squeeze out the needed drops. Put the toothpick back into the hole and slip the lemon into a small plastic bag before putting it back into the refrigerator. This way, the lemon will not dry out but will remain fresh until it is needed again.

Did you know that dampness and heat will deteriorate *instant coffee?* Store this product in a cool place, such as your refrigerator, and keep the top tightly in place.

Make your own *croutons* from day-old bread. You can use them for snacks, in soups, stewed tomatoes, and salads. Butter each slice lightly and sprinkle with paprika and onion salt, and a bit of grated cheese. Then cut each slice into small cubes, place on a cookie sheet and toast in the oven. Store the croutons in a tightly covered container.

Or drain your bacon on the dry slices. You can then cut them into small cubes and toast them in a 225 degree oven for tasty croutons.

Cold roast beef will stay moist and tasty if you wrap it in a dampened piece of cheesecloth while it is still warm. Try it.

Don't let those *marshmallows* dry out. When you open the bag and use only a small portion of it, freeze the rest. It won't take long for the marshmallows to defrost when needed again, and if you find it necessary to cut them up for use in a recipe, it is a lot easier to slice them while still frozen.

Especially during *summer months*, you will find those cereal boxes which have been opened will stay fresher if a plastic bag is put over the top. Sandwich-size plastic bags are also great for encasing opened boxes of baking soda, raisins, etc., during those months when the humidity soars.

Cookies can be kept fresh in a cookie jar by adding a slice of fresh bread every other day.

Drop cookies can be freshened by heating them in a covered casserole in a slow oven for about 20 minutes. If the cookies you would like to freshen are of the crispier variety, place them on a cookie sheet and leave them in a slow oven for approximately 10 minutes.

Cooking Substitutes

Here is a satisfactory substitute for *hollandaise:* Add the juice of one lemon to a half cup of mayonnaise.

If you don't have a *cake cover*, why not invert a large mixing bowl over your layer cake to keep it covered and fresh?

Try tasty cottage cheese and chives as a change from *sour cream* topping for baked potatoes. Less expensive, fewer calories, and it gives your protein intake a boost! Buttermilk is another tasty substitute for sour cream.

Cream cheese is an excellent substitute for butter or margarine when making a confectioners' sugar frosting. If the mixture is a little thick, thin it with milk or fruit juice.

Did you know that a teaspoon and a half of *cornstarch* equals a tablespoon of flour in thickening power?

Buttermilk is a good substitute for *cream of tartar*. If it isn't sour enough, add a little vinegar.

If you like to take a slice off that food budget by making your own *butter*, blenders are the greatest invention since cream. Fill the blender about three-fourths full of cream, put the lid on, switch to low speed and let it churn. The motor will change its tone when the butter begins to gather. You will then know it is time to take your rubber scraper and carefully push the thick cream down and away from the sides. Pour the butter into a larger container with a strainer, and spray it thoroughly but gently with the spray on the kitchen tap, to rinse away the remaining milk. Wash and wash and wash until every drop of moisture is out of the butter. Salt sparingly but according to taste, mold it, and serve it with pride.

By the way, if you don't want to get your spatulas ground up when using them in the blender, put the spatula in just far enough to clear the blades, then mark that point on the handle with dry marking pen, nail polish, or anything that will not wash off. You will always know just how far the spatula can safely go into the blender.

No fresh *gingerroot* in your house when the recipe calls for it? Simmer a dried gingerroot in water for about 10 minutes and use that. The dehydrated ginger should be used soon after it is softened.

If you run out of *baking powder* you can combine cream of tartar and baking soda for a similar effect. Use one-fourth teaspoon of soda plus one-half teaspoon of cream of tartar as a substitue for one teaspoon of baking powder.

Ideas for Leftovers

Save those leftover *cookie and cake crumbs* in a jar in your refrigerator. When you have enough accumulated you can use them for a quick pie crust or a topping for ice cream, or for those canned fruit desserts. If you use them for a pie crust, just follow your favorite graham cracker crust recipe, substituting the crumbs for the graham crackers.

That *hardened cheese* can be grated and used in sauces, omelets, etc. Store it in the refrigerator in a covered container until you are ready to use it.

Egg whites as well as yolks will keep well when stored in the refrigerator in a *margarine tub*. Individual servings of salad will also be kept from wilting when stored in this manner. Margarine tubs are also good for odor-free keeping of sliced onion halves or your leftover bacon grease (be sure the grease has cooled before pouring into the plastic container).

Does your family enjoy fried *potato cakes* made from leftover mashed potatoes? If so, store the leftover potatoes in the refrigerator in a straight-sided glass tumbler. Then, when you are ready to fix the potato cakes, you can run a knife around the potato cylinder to remove it in one solid piece. It will be ready to slice into nicely shaped potato cakes.

Did you forget to leave the milkman a note saying, "No milk today"? *Milk*, when frozen in a paper carton, will stay in good condition for several months. However, when you take it out of the freezer and it begins to thaw, stir it a few times to help keep it smooth.

When going on a trip, pour any milk you have on hand in your ice cube tray and freeze it. When you get home all you have to do is thaw it out and you are saved a trip to the store.

Here is a recipe for a *leftover fowl* such as chicken, turkey, or duck. Cut the meat slices into bite-size pieces. Add cooked spaghetti, green peppers, and slivered almonds. Place the mixture in a greased baking dish. Cover the top with grated cheese and bread crumbs. Bake in a moderate oven until the top is brown.

When baking *pies*, make tart-size ones from the leftover crust and filling for your husband's or the children's lunch boxes.

Don't throw out leftover *bacon*. Fry it a little more, if

necessary, to make it very crisp, then crumble it into peanut butter for a yummy sandwich spread.

When only part of a package of *marshmallows* is left over, don't let them get stale and hard. Cut the marshmallows into small pieces and soak them in orange juice for about a half hour. Break peanut brittle into this mixture and fold in whipped cream. Place in the freezer for several hours for a delightful dessert.

Did you know that *butter and margarine wrappers* are excellent for buttering the tops of brown 'n serve rolls before baking?

Looking for a different way to serve that economical food—*rice?* Stir in grated Parmesan or Romano cheese and strips of canned pimento. This is especially delicious as a side dish served with veal.

If you really want to get that last bit of *salad dressing* out of the bottle, set it in a pan of hot water for a few minutes. It will come out easily.

Save the brines from *pickles.* Add vegetables such as carrots, cabbage, celery, beans, peas, and cauliflower to the brine and place in the refrigerator. By adding oil and seasonings, you will have a delicious vegetable salad.

Don't throw away the leaves that top your *celery* stalks. Put them on a foil-covered cookie sheet and place them in an unlighted oven until they dry out. It make take a few days, so when you use the oven take out your celery tops, then replace them when the oven has cooled off a bit. When they are crunchy, fold the foil into a bag and you will have a marvelous celery seasoning for your stews, soups, and gravies.

Or chop the celery tops finely and add them to your homemade barbecue sauce.

For a different gourmet taste, take the leftover *juice* from any canned fruit and use it to baste broiled poultry.

When there are a few cooked *frankfurters* left over, use them as a sandwich filling. Chop the franks fine and add pickle relish and salad dressing.

Sandwich leftover *ham* between two squares of hot corn bread and top the sandwich with cheese. Watch your family go for it!

Tips on Produce

For a fast way to remove silk from *corn ears*, rub them with dry terrycloth towel. They will then be ready to rinse and cook.

Do you think of grinding *cranberries* as an unpleasant, juicy job? They will grind very neatly when frozen. Wash the berries, pat them dry, and freeze in plastic bags until you are ready to grind them.

To keep your house livable while cooking *cabbage*, put a heel of bread on top of the cabbage while cooking. It absorbs the odors!

Did you know that the outer leaves of *leafy greens* are the richest in calcium, iron, and Vitamin A? If they are too tough for salads, add them to your soups.

To ripen *tomatoes* quickly, put them in a plastic bag with a very ripe apple. Punch a few holes in the bag, and place it where the temperature will be about 70 degrees (such as in a cabinet). They will ripen more slowly in the refrigerator.

Spinach fresh from the garden requires fewer washings

if the first washing has three tablespoons of salt in the water.

If the larger *eggs* cost 7 cents or more more than the smaller ones, you will save money if you buy the smaller ones.

Ever wonder how many *apples* you can count on when you buy by the pound? You can gauge it this way: four small, three medium, or two large apples usually amount to about a pound. As with meats and other foods sold by weight, it is the number of servings in a unit package (i.e., here, the number of apples in a bag) that determines the value you get for your money, not the number of pounds.

Wondering how to keep those tasty apples through the winter without a dirt-floor cellar? Experts say the closer you keep them to 32 degrees, the longer they will last. So the refrigerator is fine. Use a cool basement or garage for larger amounts.

Wilted *lettuce or celery* can be freshened if you stand it in cold water for about ten minutes.

If your garden has yielded a bumper crop of *potatoes* to be stored over winter, follow the advice of the U.S. Department of Agriculture. Spread them out for a week in a well-ventilated garage (out of the sun) to condition them for long keeping. Then keep them in a dark, unheated area that is humid and well ventilated, with a temperature between 40 and 50 degrees.

Baking

If you want to avoid artificial food colorings in your *Halloween baking*, add grated carrot to the sugar glaze. The cookies will come out bright orange and will taste just the way they always did.

For a quick way to slice a roll of *refrigerator cookies*, use your cheese slicer. The cookies will be uniform in size and pretty.

To cut *candied fruits* and dates more easily for holiday baking, dip your scissors often in hot water.

When the holiday season is about over, buy glacéd fruits on sale. Stock up on them for next year's baking and store them in plastic bags in your freezer.

When baking, most of us have leftover *frosting* that is too little to save for another cake, yet too much to throw away. Spread the frosting between two graham crackers and place each sandwich in a plastic bag. Close tightly and freeze for snacks for the children with a glass of milk—or for adults with a cup of tea.

Even though sugar prices may have dropped in your area, commercially baked goods remain expensive because packaging and labor costs have gone up. So, it will really pay you to bake your own *holiday cookies*. All you need is a good recipe. Make your own frostings, too. Prepared frostings cost about four times as much as homemade. A tin of homemade cookies is always a most welcome gift.

Coffee and Other Beverages

Consumer experts suggest we save money by grinding our own *coffee beans*. Not only do beans cost less than comparable vacuum-packed ground coffee, but they keep their flavor longer! At today's coffee prices an electric grinder could pay for itself in a short while. Watch for sales on coffee beans. Toasted beans can be successfully stored in the freezer for months. Defrosting before use is unnecessary. So, if you have your morning java every day, buy coffee beans and grind out some savings.

Here is another way to save that high-priced coffee. Place that *leftover* coffee in a glass in the refrigerator. Then, when you are in a hurry in the morning and pour cups of coffee that are too hot to handle, the cold coffee stored in the refrigerator will be the solution to cool it to drinking temperature without diluting it.

You can also save on ground coffee by using a *fine grind* with a drip pot and, of course, a paper filter. Experiment with the amount of ground coffee needed to obtain the strength that suits you. Since the fine-grind coffee makes a stronger brew, you use less for each pot. There are also 1 ½ more scoops in a pound of fine-grind coffee than there are in a pound of regular grind.

If you use the *drip method* of making coffee, you can easily get eight cups for the price of six. Place in the filter the amount of coffee you should use for six cups. Pour in three cups of hot water. Allow it to drip through completely, then add three more cups of water and allow that to drip through. Finally, add two more cups of hot water. You will end up with eight cups with no difference in taste.

If you own a *microwave oven*, leftover morning coffee can be reheated in the oven during the day and comes out tasting like fresh-perked!

When struggling with your beverage budget, note that one pound of *tea* makes about 200 cups, and one pound of coffee makes only 50 cups!

If your family drinks a lot of *Kool-Aid* in the summer, those plastic milk jugs are perfect containers and provide an easy way to make it. After washing and rinsing the jug thoroughly, put the Kool-Aid, sugar, and water in the jug, screw on the cap and shake it. No stirring will be necessary.

A festive *punch* can be made from ginger ale and fruit-flavored sherbet. You might want to add a little grapefruit juice and "spirits."

A lovely addition to this beverage is fruited ice cubes. Into each cube section place one red cherry, one green cherry, a mandarin orange slice, and a grapefruit slice. Add water and freeze.

The nonalcoholic ingredients for your holiday punch can also be frozen and used as ice cubes. This will prevent watering down the beverage. Why not use round containers—such as margarine or cottage cheese cartons —for freezing?

Canning

In the fall, canning should save us a lot of money. But all the work isn't worth anything if the product doesn't come out the way you want it to, or if there is any possible danger.

The National Canners' Association gives these words of advice:

After your jars are cooled, check the *seal* following the instructions given by the manufacturer. If you find a leaky jar, use unspoiled food right away. Store the rest of the foods in a dark, cool, dry place.

Never taste or serve *questionable products*. Examine the products before using to be sure the liquid is clear, the color is right, the container has not leaked, and the lid has not bulged. Unless you are absolutely sure of your gauge and canning methods, boil home-canned vegetables before tasting. The heating usually makes any odor or spoilage more evident. Spinach and corn should be boiled 20 minutes. If the food looks spoiled, foams, or has an off-odor while heating, destroy it. Any spoons or other utensils used in emptying the food into the saucepan should receive the same heat treatment. Bring to a boil, then cover and boil at least 10 minutes.

Miscellaneous Tips on Food

When making *carry-out lunches*, try using your pan-cake turner for transferring gooey, drippy sandwiches such as chicken salad from the counter to the sandwich bag. It works beautifully!

You *can* toast that *frosted raisin bread* in your pop-up toaster without danger of the frosting melting and gumming up the mechanism. Stick a metal skewer horizontally through two slices of bread, near the frosting. This will prevent them from sliding into the toaster all the way, leaving the frosted section sticking up over the top of the toaster.

Did you know how many hidden talents a box of *baking soda* has? When added to water it can: soak dried beans to make them more digestible, remove the "gamey" taste from wild game, sweeten sour dishcloths, brighten jewelry, or clean a scorched enamel pan. Dry soda can: clean grease spatters from the stove and cooking area, and scour sinks and tubs. And soda paste can reduce itching from insect bites.

Here is another use for those handy foil *oven liners*. They can be used as cookie sheets when you are baking a large batch. They will save you lots of oven time and energy.

One way to cut the cost of cheese-based *salad dressings*, especially the creamy kinds, is to mix in a small amount of cottage cheese, Roquefort, bleu, or other strong cheese to impart their flavor to the lower-priced cheese.

Freeze that *fresh fish* in *water*. Then, when you thaw the fish to cook, use the water on your house plants—for a very good fertilizer.

Here is a quick way to take the skin off frozen fish. Hold the fish skin side up for a few seconds under hot water immediately after removing from the freezer. The skin will peel off just as easily as if you were peeling a banana.

When *scaling fish* indoors, place a plastic bag in the sink, large enough to hold the fish, your hands, and the scaling knife. You can then easily see what you are doing through the plastic, and nary a scale flies onto the floor, keeping the mess at a minimum.

When using a *double boiler*, the food in the top saucepan will cook very much faster if a little salt is added to the water in the lower pan.

For those of us who have ever been burned by *chicken livers* popping while frying, here is a simple trick. Pierce the livers well with a fork before frying—and you can relax.

Here is an idea for a simply-made, inexpensive, and colorful *garnish* for your meat trays. Cut peeled lemons into ¼-inch slices, making sure to remove all the white pith before you slice them. Discard the seeds. Roll half the edge of each slice in finely minced parsley, and the other half in paprika for a truly lovely decoration.

For all *Melba toast* lovers, here is an easy and inexpensive way to make your own. Freeze brown-and-serve rolls so that you can slice them very thin with an electric knife. Bake at 325 degrees for 15 to 20 minutes, checking to get the degree of browness you desire. If you can pick up the rolls at a thrift bakery, you will save even more!

With rising food costs, most cheese has become quite expensive. *Cheddar cheese soup* could be your answer. Pour it over baked potatoes, put it on top of English muffins, hamburger patties, macaroni, or even apple pie.

Mild *cheddar cheese* can do double duty if you know how to convert it to sharp cheddar for special recipes. Add dry mustard and Worcestershire sauce to taste, and you will have a very acceptable sharp cheese.

Your *coffee pot* makes a dandy asparagus cooker. Tie a bunch of asparagus together and stand it up in the pot. This keeps the tips from breaking. Fill the pot half full with water and cover. The steam will tenderly cook the tips.

A *grapefruit knife* is dandy for removing the tops and seeds of green and red peppers . . . without slicing into the sides.

To cut *hard butter*, cover the blade of a knife with waxed paper. It will slice cleanly.

Those *nylon scrubbers* are wonderful for cleaning sweet potatoes and white potatoes before baking.

When all your *freezer containers* are filled, there is no need to go out and buy more. Run a little warm water over the bottom of each container as you remove it from the freezer. The contents will pop out in a solid mass. Immediately place each block in a plastic bag and secure it air tight with a twist tie. Put them back into the freezer before they have thawed. Now your containers are all ready to use again.

A gorgeous Christmas plum pudding may be waiting to be steamed—but what will you use as a *steamer*? A deep kettle will work if you use an empty can as a stand to keep the pudding dry.

During the holidays when your refrigerator is overloaded, remember picnic hampers and *cold chests*, packed with ice, can keep those party foods cold for many hours.

A long-handled *potato peeler* is a dandy gadget for removing the hulls from strawberries.

Here is another use for your *garlic press*. Crush bouillon cubes, still in their foil wrappers, in the press. The cubes will dissolve much more quickly in boiling water.

Use a *pizza cutter* instead of a knife to slice brownies and one-layer cakes while still warm. It quickly makes neat slices.

You won't scratch your pizza pan if you use your *kitchen shears* to cut the pizza. Gently lift the pizza with a spatula and cut the desired size with shears that are sharp.

That *nutcracker* is handy when opening sticky screw-type bottles and jars, such as salad oils, pancake syrup, molasses, and cough syrups. It even works when a bottle of nail polish refuses to open.

A *beer can opener* is a dandy tool to use for deveining shrimp quickly and effortlessly.

Keep *ice trays* from sticking to shelves of your freezing compartment by putting aluminum foil or wax paper underneath the trays before inserting.

Wouldn't it be lovely if all manufacturers marked the size on the bottom of their *baking dishes?* For those not marked, use this rule of thumb. A one-quart casserole will hold four cups of water, 1 ½ quarts will hold six cups, etc.

An extra-long cord on your kitchen *telephone* can be one of your greatest time savers. Many tasks can be easily done during most telephone conversations—such as wiping the counter,rearranging cupboards, fixing the salad for dinner, or even stirring up a cake. A telephone shoulder rest will leave both hands free for these mini-jobs.

fluffy and high if you use quick-cooking tapioca instead of flour to thicken the milk base. Three tablespoons to one cup of milk for a three-egg soufflé is just about right.

A temporary *broiler pan* can very easily be fashioned by crumpling heavy aluminum foil and placing it in a shallow baking pan. The creases in the foil will catch the drippings adequately.

When the *wax paper* isn't wide enough to do the job you have for it, you can increase the width easily by pressing two pieces together with a warm iron.

Do you hesitate to install a costly *paper toweling rack*, or have you no space for one? Why not slide the roll onto the curtain rod at the window above your sink? The paper toweling will be convenient, saving you time and steps, yet costing not a penny.

If you find you have misplaced those *turkey skewers* or poultry nails, put a raw, peeled potato in the opening at either end of the bird to hold the stuffing. When the turkey is done, you will find the potatoes are roasted and the stuffing is still intact.

Make it a rule to protect your *cookout charcoal* this summer so that it will start easily. Once the package has been opened, store it in a large plastic bag or a container with a tight lid so that the moisture cannot be absorbed.

An ordinary waxed empty milk carton is a good *charcoal lighter*. Fill with coals and lay on its side on the grill. Start the lower side burning, and no fuel lighter will be needed. When the container is burned, the coals will be white, hot, and ready to use.

You can also make your own starters for the campfire or cookout by inserting a charcoal briquet in each section of a cardboard (not plastic) egg carton. Melt paraffin and pour over the briquets. Allow to cool, then cut the carton sections apart. You will now have one dozen fire starters.

Make *logs* for your fireplace out of those old newspapers. Roll the newspapers very tightly (you can buy a special roller expressly for this job), and slip heavy rubber bands over the ends and the middle to keep the rolls tight. The rolls should then be thoroughly soaked in water and put out to dry in the sun or somewhere warm. Make sure they are log size and bone dry before using.

Or, fold sections of the papers as long as you want and about ¼ inch thick. Immerse completely in detergent water overnight, using about the same amount of detergent as you would for dishwashing. The next morning, roll each package of newspapers tightly on a broomstick, kneading as you roll, to compress the papers into a compact log. Slip each paper log from the stick and place it on end to dry. Tie each end with wire to prevent unrolling. Depending on heat and humidity, it will take from one to three weeks for your logs to dry enough to burn.

Need another good *fire starter* for your fireplace? Try draining fried foods onto brown paper bags. Don't throw the bags out. After they have been saturated, keep them handy until the time comes to start your evening fire—then put a match to the paper. The cooking and food oils will flame up immediately.

Those packaged *fireplace logs* you see for sale in supermarkets are expensive (and can be unsafe) when used whole. Cut up, however, they make good fire starters for real logs. Use a serrated knife to cut up a log into inch-thick sections, and place a section under the kindling when you lay a fire. Lit, it will start your fire easily. Store unused sections in plastic bags to keep them from drying out.

Don't ever use your fireplace as an incinerator for

burning *newspapers!* The sudden intense heat could cause the chimney soot to catch fire.

When you run out of *freezer tape,* masking tape is a good substitute. It not only adheres very well, but it is cheaper.

There is no need to keep a box of seldom-used *cake flour* on your shelf. When the mood strikes you to bake a cake from scratch, just add one tablespoon of cornstarch to every pound of flour and sift three times for a good substitute cake flour.

Ever have to transport many cupcakes to school, a scout meeting, etc., and find you are lacking a large enough *tray?* Scrub one of the children's snow saucers thoroughly and cover it with aluminum foil. It will become a giant tray that will carry 50 to 100 cupcakes, with room to spare.

Try wrapping two paper plates in aluminum foil to form a sturdy no-return *cake plate* you can use to carry your cake to the church bazaar, bake sale, fair, or picnic.

You can make an attractive *mat* for hot dishes by simply covering a piece of cardboard or an old magazine with foil.

If you don't have a *bread board,* wax paper can be a handy substitute. Dampen your countertop or a kitchen table with a sponge. Spread out the wax paper. The dampness will make it adhere for rolling out pie crust or kneading bread dough. By lifting the paper, you can gently pick up your dough and still have a clean table or countertop.

Household Repairs

You can replace that lost outdoor *faucet handle* with an old door knob. Position the knob where the handle was, then use two screws to hold the knob secure. It will, at least, provide you with a good faucet until you can get to the hardware store for the permanent item.

If the washer in a *leaky faucet* cannot be replaced immediately, it can simply be turned upside down. The inverted washer will work well until you are ready to buy a new one.

You can make a handy *funnel* for pouring paint into other containers, out of the top of a plastic bleach bottle. Cut the jug in half, turn upside down—and there is your funnel.

Instead of using *steel wool* when removing old varnish from a piece of furniture, try using a plastic scrubbing pad (the type that seems to be made into a long strip, then knitted into a ball). This apparatus does not wear out, the gummy old varnish can be easily shaken out, and the scrubber can be used over and over again. It won't damage the wood. Stretched out to full length, you can pull the pad back and forth across the table legs or chair legs in shoeshine-boy fashion, doing a splendid job.

No need to break your fingernails and ruin your manicure if you don't have a *tack puller*. Use an ordinary stainless steel fork. You will find the stainless steel is stronger than silver and does not bend as easily. Slip the tines of the fork under the tack—and pull.

Need a piece of *weatherstripping*? Try using adhesive-backed latex foam rubber tape. It is inexpensive and it needn't be tacked down to seal out drafts.

Masking tape and temporary caulking compounds like Mortite can also make easy and *effective seals* for cold-air leaks at windows, doors, and floorboards.

Household Items You Can Make Yourself

Ever wish you had a *cutting guide* such as fabric centers have? If you have a table that accommodates extra leaves, you have your very own cutting guide right at home. Pull the table apart, leaving about ¼ inch of space between the leaves. Place the fabric on the table. The space will guide your scissors as you cut.

Freezer paper makes inexpensive *drawer liners*. Because this paper has a waxed surface on one side, it works very well. The roll also has a cutting edge on the box, cutting down on the time required to fit the liners.

Need *white ink* for spatter-painting or writing? Use white shoe polish instead. It is not only thicker, but shows up better.

You can easily improvise a *movie screen* by using a card table which has been covered with a sheet. Open two of the legs for balance, and set the table on a chest or low table.

Save the price of an *umbrella stand* by fashioning your own. Take three large-size coffee cans and cut the bottoms out of two of them. Stack them with the one with a bottom at the bottom, and hold them together with 2-inch wide tape. Cover the whole thing with pretty paper, wallpaper, or contact paper. Clear gloss shellac can be added as extra protection for your pretty umbrella stand. Make a base for the stand from a square of plywood, 12 to 18 inches on a side.

Planning to be away for awhile this year? Here is an idea for inexpensive *dust covers* for your furnishings. Terrycloth, blind-hemmed with matching seam tape, makes excellent couch and chair throws. You will find it has a nice texture, is cool and comfortable while in use, is easily laundered, and does not "creep" as some fabrics are inclined to do. Many colors are available, or you can tint the material the same color as your upholstery fabric, avoiding that ghostly look so many dust covers have.

You can make your own soapy *bath sponge* by cutting several slots in a large sponge, then filling the slots with scraps of soap.

If you don't have any *plastic bags* to cover your clothes, an old pillow case will do the trick just as well. Make an opening at the top of the case for the hanger, and slip the case down over the clothes.

Have you misplaced your *lint brush*? Those little balls made from nylon net are excellent for cleaning lint, bits of tobacco, and such out of shirt pockets—and even for cleaning the inside linings of your purses. A wad of masking tape, sticky side out, serves the same end.

You won't have to invest in *pillow covers* if you put your older pillow cases on the pillows before putting on the regular pair. They will not only protect your pillow tickings, but will make your cases look whiter if the ticking is striped or colored.

If a missing *thimble* causes you to put off that "stitch in time," you will be surprised to discover that some plastic bottle caps (those found on tubes of hair cream, toothpaste, etc.) are thimble-sized. Keep a collection of them in a drawer of your sewing machine. When you need one, you will find them to be an almost perfect substitute.

If you need another *key ring*, why not try a metal shower curtain clip? You will find it will hold many keys, is easy to fish out of your purse, and really stays shut.

When a *shoe polish dauber* gets broken before the

polish is gone, don't despair. A ½-inch paint brush gets into the cracks and between the shoe and sole better than the dauber ever did!

Ever lose the little white button from the *top of a spray can?* The directions on these aerosol cans warn that you must *never* puncture the can. However, you can still use the contents if you have another can handy with the same type of button. "Borrow" the cap from the other can, and chances are it will work perfectly.

A handy *cotton dispenser* can be made by placing the cotton in a small plastic bag, twisting the top and then closing the bag with a medium-size safety pin. Do not run the pin through the plastic, only around the twisted top of the bag. The top will unwind just enough so that the cotton can be pulled through the small hole the pin allows.

When you don't have an *envelope sealer* and have a lot of envelopes to moisten, an ice cube wrapped in a cloth will prove a handy gadget.

When making your own *spray starch*, cooked starch is the best to use. Pour some of this into a bottle, add water to it, and attach a spray top. The original container of cooked starch can be kept in the refrigerator until needed for refilling. You might find that this spray is not as fine as those which are commercially filled in aerosol cans. If so, remember to put a little more distance between you and the fabric you are spraying in order to get a more even result.

When you need a small *clamp*, like one used to hold a stone in a ring, take an old screw-type earring. It will work just fine!

When there is illness at your house, you can make a dandy *thermometer holder* such as is used in hospitals. Take a clean prescription bottle, stuff it with cotton saturated with alcohol. Make a hole in the cap of the bottle with an ice pick, just large enough to put the thermometer through. You will find this more convenient than returning the thermometer to the case after each use, and much more sanitary, too.

Did you know that children's play putty makes an ideal emergency cleaner for your *typewriter keys*? It picks up all the excess ink and leaves the keys shiny again. Best of all, you do not end up with inky fingers, and there is a minimum of mess involved. Just press the putty onto the keys, fold it over again, work a moment and then press again. The putty will absorb all the ink.

If you want to measure something and don't have a *ruler*, remember that a dollar bill is 6 ¼ inches long.

That key that used to open a can of ham, etc., makes an excellent emergency *screwdriver*.

When the felt wears out on those expensive *wooden pants hangers*, replace it with Moleskin and the hanger will be good as new.

When those *envelopes* won't seal, use the white of an egg. Just a tiny bit of egg white that has been left in the shell does the job quickly and effectively.

You can make a great, inexpensive *foot scraper* by nailing pop-bottle tops upside down onto heavy board. Place this on the back porch near the door, as a reminder to family members to scrape snow and mud off their boots before coming indoors.

Those fabric softener sheets that go into the clothes dryer are great *lint removers*. Keep the used ones in a small bag by the dryer. When you remove a load, clean the lint screen with them.

·4·

Dollar Stretchers for Mothers

HERE ARE SOME helpful hints for saving money on children's clothes, toys, food . . . and even parties!

For the Girls

If your little girls habitually lose those *pony tail clips*, why not use a tie band (the kind that come on plastic bags)? Pipe cleaners work equally as well in an emergency.

Here are a few ideas for the mothers who save money by sewing clothes for those 15-inch *dolls*. A piece of plastic, cut from the bottom of a bleach bottle, makes a fine hoop to make the full-skirted dresses stand out. Cut the hole in the center just large enough for the doll to fit through. A smaller piece of this plastic makes a good base for a crown-less pillbox hat to match the ensemble.

Use lightweight felt to make coats, skirts, etc., and they will need no hemming. A chin-tied bonnet or bridesmaid's hat can easily be fashioned from a piece of net gathered into about a 2-inch length and then sewn onto a 14-inch length of ribbon. Trim with flowers or fluffy feathers.

The little girls in your house will be delighted if you decorate their *doll houses* with your odd earrings. You can make chandeliers, centerpieces, etc., at no expense.

When your girls wear the knees out of their summer slacks, cut the slacks off above the knees for shorts and use the excess material to make a matching halter. A package of bias tape can be purchased for 39 cents, sewn around the halter, and used for the ties. Presto—an outfit for the rest of the summer that costs approximately 39 cents.

If your little girl loses her hat or kerchief in the cloakroom at school, why not sew a big pocket to the lining of her coat to hold her head gear? Chances are, she will enjoy using it.

Here is an idea for getting another couple of season's wear out of your girls' good *wool skirts*. When they get too short, buy bonded wool jersey in a solid matching color, and cut a long-waisted jumper top. Take the band off the skirt and sew the skirt and jumper top together. This will drop the length so that the outfit can be worn for several more seasons.

For the Boys

When decorating a small boy's room, why not use a discarded toy dump truck for a *planter*? Not only will the planter be rugged, but you will have a unique conversation piece which the child will really enjoy.

If there is a do-it-yourselfer Jr. around your house, paint a piece of pegboard to match his bedroom decor. Hang it on the wall, and he can then keep his very own *tools* handy and orderly, with less chance for loss.

Be sure to provide him with a small *magnet*. It will help to pick up the nails that he spills on the floor.

Thrifty Play Ideas

If your children have a few men missing from their *board games*, how about using a few of dad's extra golf tees to replace them?

Ordinary *corks* of various sizes make delightful bath toys for babies. You can even paint them with food coloring if you so desire.

Ever try stringing empty *spools* on a cord? Nylon parachute cord or fishing line is fine for this. You can paint the spools and make the chain about 4 feet long. You will be surprised at how much enjoyment children get from this handmade object. In their imaginations, it becomes a water hose, snake, train, etc.

Those worn spots in the *lawn* under the children's swings or slide can be effectively remedied with a rubber-link door mat. Put enough mats down to cover the worn spot, and the grass will grow between the links, holding the mat in place. A hand lawn mower will ride over them very easily.

Cut pieces of *garden hose* 18 inches long and slip them over the chains of children's swings to prevent pinched hands.

Do the little tots slip off the *backyard swing?* Try attaching those rubber flower decals—the kind sold to prevent bathtub slippage—to the seat of the swing. It will work!

You can preserve those inflatable *water toys* for the next season by washing them in lukewarm suds and then rinsing. Be sure the items are completely dry. Deflate and fold loosely. Store where it is warm to prevent cracking.

When the boys in your house have mid-winter dreams

of being out on the baseball diamond, a *plastic foam ball* is a handy thing to have around. If the ball touches the ceiling or walls, it will leave no mark. It is also light in weight, so it will cause little or no damage to furnishings.

A sponge *kneeling pad* in the bottom of a child's wagon will not only save the knees of his pants, but it will also absorb some of the bumps.

Those plastic *net bags* that hold potatoes, oranges, and onions are dandy for storing children's balls. Hang the bag from a nail in the garage or basement.

If there is a budding *artist* in your house, or a student using brushes and pencils, squeeze a plastic fruit basket (the kind that holds small tomatoes or berries) into a wide-mouth jar. The brushes and pencils will stand erect when inserted into this handy gimmick.

Here is an easy way to clean those *stuffed animals* that cannot be washed or dry-cleaned, particularly those containing a radio or music box. Use a dry shampoo and brush it out, being sure to brush out every smidgen so the baby cannot inhale the powder.

You can keep the little ones busy on a wintry "stay-in" day by creating an *indoor sandbox*. All you need is a dishpan and a 5-pound bag of cornmeal for sand. The children can use many things to play in the "sand"—spoons, measuring cups, etc. The cornmeal vacuums up quickly and it doesn't scratch the floor.

When your children's *modeling clay containers* become worn out or lost, a potato chip container is the next best thing. After use, put the clay in the potato chip can and tightly seal it with the plastic lid. The clay will stay soft and pliable through many play times.

An excellent, easily worked *modeling clay* substitute can be made from the following recipe:

1 cup salt	4 tablespoons oil
2 cups flour	4 teaspoons cream of tartar
2 cups water	food coloring

Combine ingredients over low heat, stirring constantly until the mixture becomes very stiff and comes away from the sides of the pot. Store in a closed plastic bag or other closed container.

You can quickly clean your child's *chalkboard* with vinegar. It will look like new.

An old, discarded white *window shade*, mounted on regular shade brackets in a child's room makes a dandy, inexpensive drawing screen. Pull the shade down, secure it with an eye screw and hook, and they can draw to their heart's content. Use colored chalk and a blackboard eraser to remove the drawings. Roll it up, out of the way, when it is not in use.

Wrap new *crayons* with masking tape and there will be less breakage.

Save those little *brushes* that come with nail polish. Soak in polish remover and let the little ones use them for painting small model cars or other projects.

An inexpensive and useful *toy box* can be made by putting casters or rollers on an unused dresser drawer so that it can be rolled under a bed or out of sight when not in use.

A dandy *baby toy* can be made by saving plastic lids from aerosol cans of all sizes and colors. Make a hole in the center of each lid by heating a nail on the stove burner. (Be sure to hold the hot nail with pliers.) Several lids can then be strung on a cord to make a gay and noisy toy which can be hung in the playpen where baby can either watch it or hit it.

Save all those plastic food containers and turn them into toys for the *sandbox* set. After washing them thoroughly, cut the containers into various shapes and make bowls, dishes, scoops, funnels, pails, shovels, etc. They make excellent toys for outdoor play as there are no sharp edges and they can be left in the sandbox without danger of rusting.

Every tot can have an *artist's smock* to protect his clothing while painting, playing with clay, and doing other creative—but messy—projects. Take a worn man's work shirt, cut off the collar and sleeves, and shorten the shirt to the desired length. Then put in the hems and have the child wear it backwards.

If some of your toddler's toys do not have balls on the ends of the *pull cords* to help them hold them, save those snap-on tops from liquid detergent bottles. Run the cord through a hole in the top, then tie the knot to hold it. Now that he has something to hold onto, he will enjoy his toys much more.

There is nothing like an *abacus* for helping a child learn to count. You can make a simple little abacus for your preschool child in the following manner: Clip the lower edge of a coat hanger with wire snippers, bend the side into a hook and slip spools onto the lower bar of the hanger. You may paint the spools if you like. Close the hook (covered with tape for safety), and your child can learn to count to five or so, as well as do simple addition and subtraction, by sliding the spools back and forth.

Do your children enjoy playing with *jigsaw puzzles?*

Mixed, scattered, and lost pieces needn't be a regular oc-
currence at your house if you take a magic marker pen and
place an identifying letter on the back of each piece of
every puzzle. All the parts of the Red Riding Hood puzzle,
for example, could be marked with an "R." The children
can then sort the pieces quickly, and they will enjoy reading
off the letters.

When those jigsaw *puzzle boxes* break, use plastic ice
cream cartons with close-fitting tops for storing the puzzles.
You can paste the puzzle picture or part of it on the top for
identification.

Save your small pieces of *leftover soap* and let the
children carve them with blunt butter knives. They can
make cute little animals or flowers from them, then use
them as their very own bars of soap. Not only will mother
be economizing, but there is a good chance that the child
will use a bit more soap than he otherwise would.

There are several methods of making paints for *finger
painting*. Liquid starch works well, as does ordinary
wallpaper paste mixed to a thick consistency. Have the
children mix powdered paint into whichever base you
choose, then put the paint in small jars with holes in the
top. You can then shake the paint onto the paper after
spreading water on it. Both are easy to clean up if they
happen to spill.

Here is a finger paint recipe used in many homes and
schools:

1½ c. starch	2 T. glycerine
4 c. boiling water	food coloring
1½ c. soap flakes	

Mix the starch with enough cold water to make a paste.
Add boiling water slowly, stirring constantly. Cook until
clear. Avoid too hot a fire. Stir in soap flakes while still
warm. Add glycerine when cooked. Add food coloring to the

amount you will be using right away, and store the remainder in the refrigerator in a covered jar.

These paints work best on glazed paper, such as shelf paper.

Clothing Care Tricks

If you forget to take along that all-important *bib* for baby, why not snap a clean pair of plastic pants around his neck? You will find they cover the child from the neck to the waist, providing you with one of the most efficient "bibs" you have ever used!

When it is necessary to use a *safety pin* as a temporary measure on children's clothing, it is safest to use a diaper pin, as they are designed not to be easily opened.

Use dental floss to sew on children's *buttons*, for strong, long-lasting wear.

When your "little kittens" lose a *mitten*, save the odd ones. Fit them inside matched mittens for extra warmth on stormy days.

Those of us who have stairs often put things to be put away on the staircase in hope that the owners will pick them up on their way upstairs. But it doesn't always work that way. At our house we have a *"Stairway Witch"* who swoops down at night and scoops up everything that's left into a shopping bag and hides it. It doesn't take many such strikes to convince your family to pick up their things more promptly.

Those *leotards* children wear seem useless when they develop a run in them. However, you can make stretch panties out of them. Cut them above the knee and sew cotton lace around the leg, pulling the stretch material slightly as you sew to prevent binding the legs.

When taking your children to museums, movies, etc. in the wintertime, why not take along a plastic *shopping bag?* When you check their coats you can put all the hats, scarves, and mittens in the bag and give the bag to the checker to hang on a hanger with your coats. This way, you won't misplace a thing.

Sew a small pocket of terrycloth on the corner of your child's *beach towel.* Attach a piece of Velcro fastener across the inside top of the pocket. This provides a safe place for the child's snack money when he goes to the pool or the beach. A larger pocket could also hold sun glasses.

While you are readying school clothes for your little tyke, sew a loop of elastic thread inside each *sweater cuff.* Slip this loop over the child's thumb when you pull a jacket over the sweater and the sweater sleeves will not roll up.

Use an old nylon stocking as a *laundry bag* when washing baby's stockings by machine. Put a few pairs into the stocking and knot the open end. You won't have to grope for the little socks when unloading.

If you don't have a *diaper bag* for baby, why not use a small, sturdy train case? You will find that his bottles and food jars can stand upright and there is also room for a blanket, extra clothing, and possibly a favorite stuffed toy. Everything will be in plain sight as soon as the bag is opened. You might find the train case is handier to work out of than most diaper bags.

When you accidentally ruin the adhesive tab on a baby's *paper diaper* by getting it wet or pulling it off completely, don't throw the diaper away. Keep a 1-inch roll of masking tape next to the diaper box. The tape does an excellent job of holding the diaper in place because it is soft, strong, and waterproof.

If your kids are chronic *mitten-losers*, try this: Attach a mitten to a long string, run the string up one sleeve of your mitten-loser's coat, across the body, and down the other sleeve. Then attach the other mitten to the end of the string. The mittens will stay "found" even when the little one shakes them off.

Here is a quick and inexpensive way to cover the *scuff marks* on your children's shoes, and it requires only a trip to the play room. Select a crayon that matches the shoe color and rub over the scarred spot. Then, rub off the excess with a tissue. This dyes and waxes the scuff mark.

When traveling with little ones, how about taking along a few *disposable bibs?* These are easy to make by taking paper placemats, cutting a slit in one end and a large hole for the child's neck. Fasten with a large safety pin. These disposable bibs can be then slipped back into the original package and stored under the front seat of your car, within easy reach.

Blankets that a child has outgrown should not be discarded. Sew them up on three sides and you have a dandy "sack" for the baby to sleep in . . . just like the sleeping bags treasured by your older children.

Those inexpensive multiple *skirt hangers* work wonders in the children's closets. They are dandy for hanging bonnets as well as pairs of mittens.

Hints on Children's Food

Junior screw-top baby food jars make wonderful spillproof *drinking cups* when a hole is punched in the lid and a drinking straw is inserted.

Does everyone at your house like poppyseed or sesame seed hamburger and hot dog *buns*, except one person? If so, you can avoid buying two kinds, yet accommodate the tastes of everyone, if you serve the child who likes them plain a sandwich made with the bottom halves of two buns containing no seeds at all. Give the two tops to someone who really enjoys them!

Do you put cold *canned drinks* in the children's lunch boxes, but find they are no longer cold at noon? Wrap each can in foil. It will keep the drinks cold, and the foil can be reused many times.

Many of us have learned the hard way that we should not send anything to school in the lunch box that we really would like to have returned—you can lose some rather expensive *food boxes* that way. However, a container is awfully nice for sending a piece of heavily frosted cake, since plain wrapping tends to stick to the frosting and allows the cake or pastry to get crushed. Why not send dessert in a plastic margarine tub? The child can then throw it away along with the plastic fork and the lunch bag. Pies, jello, and even frosted brownies can be transported without crushing with these handy margarine tubs.

Saving and Earning Money

If your children can't seem to find their *library books* when it is time to return them, why not encourage them to make a "library box"? Find a carton just the right size and let them decorate it themselves with paints or crayons. If they keep their books in it, you will eliminate that last minute hunt, as well as the inevitable fine for overdue books.

Perhaps your children have regular *jobs* about the house, such as making their own beds and keeping their rooms picked up, helping with the dishes, or keeping the garage straightened. And, maybe you are the type of parent who does not believe in paying the children to do these jobs—or giving them an allowance. If so, there is still another way you can have them earn extra spending money. One housewife and mother we know posts a list on her bulletin board each week. On the list she itemizes "extra" duties for the children to perform. The list reads something like this: "Entertain the baby while I do the ironing—10 cents; Be my errand runner for the week—20 cents; Pick up the baby's toys at bedtime each night—20 cents. Please initial only three items; check the item off when the work is finished and I will pay off on Sunday morning."

Some parents choose the following method of teaching their children the economic facts of life. They establish a *family fund* for trips, parties, dinners out—whatever events the entire family enjoys. Then, each member of the family contributes to the fund. The little ones earn money for the fund by doing odd jobs. A homemade treasure chest or large piggy bank holds the contributions.

How many of us are giving our children the advantage of expensive *music lessons*, yet have to nag at them to practice? The "message" usually comes through loud and clear if they manage to get in on the paying end once in a while. Here's how one mother works it. She figures out what the lesson practice is worth in dollars and cents—in relation to what the lessons cost. Each child marks down his practice time daily. It takes eight hours of practice time to be ready for a $4 lesson. So, any week one of them does not practice his eight hours, he pays 50 cents for each hour missed, and this goes toward paying for the next lesson. Their "fines" come out of their allowances. You'd be surprised at how well the system works.

Many manufacturers who advertise in the newspapers

have *coupons* that can be redeemed for cash when you send in proof-of-purchase labels. Why not send in the names of little friends of yours? It's an economical way to provide little surprises for them. All children like to receive mail, and when there is money in it, it is an added treat!

Tips on Infant and Toddler Care

An effective and inexpensive way to keep toddlers out of *kitchen cabinets* is to secure the doors with shower curtain hooks . . . the kind that snap shut. Interlock two of these hooks to the handles of the cabinets.

The next time you travel by car with an infant, hang a *shoe bag* from the back of your front seat. The little pockets are perfect for holding bottles, diapers, powder, toys . . . all you'll need until you arrive at your destination.

Here is a step-saver for mother. Attach an *extra handle* near the bottom of each screen door so that the smallest member of the family can open doors without help.

Cleaning a child's *high chair* can be a tedious job. Remove the padded seat cushion and give the whole thing a hot shower in the shower stall, then wipe dry. Spatters of food will rinse away.

Here is a dandy way to prevent youngsters from standing up in the *shopping cart* in the supermarket. Bring along a belt and "seat belt" him into the cart. This will not only save your nervous system, it will provide more discipline in the store.

An inexpensive *screen door* on the nursery will enable mother to hear the baby, yet keep the pet dog or cat away.

When it is time to take down a crib, light fixtures, etc.,

put the *screws* to each item in a cellophane sandwich bag and tape or tie the bag to the fixture to prevent loss.

When Your Child Is Sick

When your children are bothered with *prickly heat* during the hot summer months, the itching can be put to an abrupt end if you daub the area liberally with cider vinegar. The kids may smell like a pickle barrel, but the relief is usually worth it.

Here is a dandy gift for a child who is convalescing from an illness. Rather than flowers or a plant, a bowl containing two *goldfish* will give him a great deal of pleasure, and fish live longer than cut flowers. Be sure to include a packet of fish food. Many happy hours will be spent watching the little fish cavort.

If your children have trouble taking *pills*, roll the pills lightly in butter, and they will go down easily without choking. They will taste better, too.

If a child cries because he doesn't want to take *bitter medicine*, give him a piece of ice to chew on. Once his tongue is cold, the medicine will taste better.

A placemat placed on a good-sized bread board becomes a fine *lap tray* for the older child who is confined to bed. It also becomes a good base for drawing and reading if no bed tray is available.

On your phone, or next to the fire department number in your telephone book, it is a good idea to put one of your own *address stickers*. In this way, a baby-sitter or a flustered person will know the correct address to give in case of a fire or other emergency.

Parties and Holidays

After a child's birthday party, what do you do with the *cards?* Staple them to a large piece of cardboard and fashion a collage to hang in his room.

Buy small *candy canes* to use as stirrers for hot chocolate during the holidays. The kids will love them. A cinnamon stick is a fine stirrer for the adults' hot choloate and imparts a delicate flavor as well.

That colander can become a *centerpiece* for children's parties, when colorful lollipops are inserted into the holes.

Make a children's party bright and gay with balloon *place cards*. Write the names directly on the balloons with felt-tipped markers, inflate and tie with strings placed between the fork tines at the table.

Planning a Halloween party for the children? Start the fun early by sending out eerie *invitations* in invisible ink. First write "Iron Me" in real ink. Then dip your pen in lemon juice and write your invitations. The lemon juice residue will turn brown when heated with an iron, and your ghostly message will be revealed.

Pour melted paraffin into the *pumpkin* after you have scooped it out and carved the jack-o'-lantern features. The pumpkin will last much longer.

Have you ever made *jack-o'-lantern favors* out of oranges? Cut the top off the orange to form the cover. Insert a small piece of green pipe cleaner in the top to form the stem. Remove the pulp from inside the orange. Cut eyes, nose, and a mouth in the orange shell with a pointed knife. Cut a hole from a base of a small candle to fit into the bottom of the shell and you have as many little pumpkin favors as you wish.

Your children will love homemade "Easter basket" cupcakes. Frost cupcakes made from your favorite recipe, and sprinkle coconut which has been tinted with green food coloring on top for grass. A few jelly beans on top of the coconut will be the "eggs." Bend a pipe cleaner and place it on the outer rim of each cupcake for the handle, completing a delicious and pretty basket of goodies.

Save those cottage cheese containers and make adorable *party hats* from them for that next children's party. Paste different shades of colored crepe paper on the cartons, punch holes at either side, and use string or ribbon for ties. For a Valentine's Day party, let your cherub cut out hearts, etc., to be pasted onto these hats. Birthday hats can be decorated with animal cutouts, etc.

·5·

Holiday Decorating Tricks To Fit Any Budget

THIS CHAPTER contains a bundle of tricks to make your Christmas holidays brighter—and less expensive.

Ornaments and Decorations

This coming year, why not suggest to all new brides to save the *bows* from their shower and wedding gifts to be used as inexpensive and very impressive ornaments for their first Christmas tree? Tree lights will be the only additional trimmings needed. They will always remember that first Christmas tree!

Many homemakers save those tube-like containers that ready-to-bake *biscuits* come in. By next Christmas you can have enough to make into attractive tree ornaments. The disks at the ends are easily punched to hang shimmering on the tree, or used behind the lights as reflectors. The entire container, which is usually lined with bright foil, can be pulled apart to form an attractive spiral.

If you have trouble with the lights on your *outdoor Christmas trees* blowing down, try using the plastic, snap-type clothespins to secure them to the trees. They will hold fast, no matter how hard the wind blows.

Here is another idea for those outdoor lighted trees. Run the wire leading to the electrical socket through an old garden hose laid along the ground. The wind will not loosen it, and it can be walked on without danger. The old hose can even be rolled and stored with your Christmas lights for next year.

If a Christmas tree ornament should happen to *break*, dampen a wad of cotton to pick up all the tiny particles of glass. Those cotton balls found in the tops of pill and vitamin bottles are perfect for this chore.

When your Christmas tree turns out to be a lot bigger than you expected, and you suddenly find you are short of ornaments, don't overlook the good old-fashioned custom of *stringing popcorn and cranberries*. These festive garlands can keep the children busy for hours, filling in a sparsely decorated tree inexpensively and to perfection!

When buying a fresh *Christmas tree*, you can't judge the freshness by the color. Many trees are sprayed with green dye. The experts tell us to test the tree by running your fingers along a branch. If the needles are pliable and do not pop off, you probably have a fresh tree. Also, bounce the tree several times as you inspect it. If a sprinkling of needles falls to the ground, choose another tree. If the small twigs of the tree are brittle, the tree is dried out.

When you bring a fresh tree home, cut about 2 inches off the bottom and place it in a bucket of water in a protected place until you are ready to bring it indoors.

If you are buying a new tree stand—don't scrimp. Buy

a big, sturdy one that will hold a lot of water. Set up the tree in an area that is away from heat, and not near an exit. (Should the tree burst into flames, it could fall and block the exit.)

When *"undecorating" the Christmas tree*, wear a pair of washable cotton gloves. Then, as you remove each ornament, you can gently dust it before wrapping it in tissue or paper toweling for storage. Your ornaments will be shiny and bright for next year's tree.

Are you still struggling to get the *tape* off your windows from the holiday decorations? Spray prewash laundry spot remover on the tape and watch it peel off in a jiffy.

Do you enjoy decorating the windows for the holidays with *spray-on snow* but find it is a job to get the snow off? Rub Glass Wax on the windows first and then spray on the snow. When you are ready to remove the snow, just wipe the window with a cloth and the snow comes off easily.

Here is a dandy way to make decorative "snow" to ensure a white Christmas inside as well as out. Mix 1 cup of detergent granules with ¼ cup of liquid plastic-type starch. Add a few drops of water and beat with an eggbeater until the "snow" looks like thick marshmallow cream. A drop or two of blue food coloring, or laundry bluing, will add that icy look. If you are going to use the snow to decorate your tree, you might have to make several batches. It can be easily applied if you use a clean paintbrush, but do so before stringing the lights or hanging your ornaments.

If you find you are short of ornaments and have some "snow" left over, *make* extra ornaments for the tree by dipping various objects into the snowy mixture and hanging them up to dry. Pretty decorations can be made in this way out of corks, old shower curtain rings, pencil stubs, flashbulbs, clothespins, almost any small item. A little glitter sprinkled onto the finished product adds sparkle.

Did you forget to buy a Christmas *door wreath?* You can make one quite simply by bending a wire coathanger into a round shape. Cover the wire with red or green tape and secure Christmas greens (evergreen branches, holly, or trimmings off the Christmas tree will do nicely) to the circle with thin wire or pipe cleaners. Attach a few Christmas tree ornaments and, perhaps, a few tiny bells.

Holiday is kissing time, so don't forget to get some *mistletoe*! Two embroidery hoops can make a pretty sphere in which to hang it. Cover one hoop with red ribbon and the other with green. Intersect the hoops and tie a big Christmas bow at the top, allowing the mistletoe to dangle within this sphere you have fashioned.

Some homemakers use plastic berry baskets for encasing the mistletoe. Two of these baskets placed face to face around it can be easily secured with pipe cleaners or Christmas tape.

Your *costume jewelry* can make a lovely Christmas centerpiece for your coffee table, or even your bedroom nightstand or dresser. Purchase a plain styrofoam cone from the local dime store and cover it with green felt. The felt can be secured with all-purpose glue. You can wind an old, discarded string of beads or pearls around this "Christmas tree" and pin on earrings, brooches, jeweled buttons, rings, and the like. Hat pins or ordinary straight pins will do a good job of holding the jewelry.

Here are a few ways to display those *Christmas cards* so that they can be enjoyed all through the holiday season. They can easily be hung from wall to ceiling without marring the paint by sticking a piece of cellophane tape—sticky side out—to the molding and the baseboard. Just press on the cards as they come through the mail.

Or, if you have a four-panel screen that isn't in use at the moment, cover it with nylon net. As the cards arrive, insert a small drapery hook in the back of each, hook the blunt end through the net, and hang them up. You can fill and open one panel of the screen at a time. When the screen has been completely covered, it can be unfolded all the way to display all the pretty cards.

Don't throw away those Christmas cards. Next season, you can cut out the small figures and paste them on cards to make name tags, place cards, and even party invitations easily and inexpensively.

Those who still have grass clippings or small pieces of straw can turn them into delightful *birds' nests* for the Christmas tree! Mold the clippings into muffin tins, spread with glue and let dry for several days. Next, glue the nest to a clip clothespin and spray with gold paint. To decorate, place jelly beans and a small bird in each nest.

White shoe polish is great for touching up old Christmas tree ornaments and for painting pine cones. It is easier to use then spray paint because the white goes just where you want it.

Why not put the berries from your Christmas *holly* in a corner of your flower bed so you will have baby holly plants next year? If the seeds have fleshy coverings, the pulp should be removed before planting. Soak in water until this covering is soft and easily washed off, before planting.

Your *house plants* provide a dandy "extra" tree to decorate. Many large house plants are ideal for holding featherweight trim, such as popcorn strings, tinsel ropes, small glass ornaments, and little Italian lights. However, don't use flocking, as it will suffocate the plant.

The new Scotch-pine *air freshener* will be a double blessing this Christmas if you place it near your artificial tree. It will give you the aroma of the real thing, while freshening the air.

Why not *gift wrap* the inside doors of your home and add to your holiday decorations? Run wide red ribbon around the door both vertically and horizontally, as though the door were a gift box. Tie a bow in the center and attach sprigs of holly or ornaments.

On top of the list for Christmas plants is the *Poinsettia*. If you should be lucky enough to receive one as a gift, there are a few things you can do to make it last as long as possible. The experts tell us that Poinsettias should be kept in bright light, but hot sun is not beneficial. They should also be kept moderately moist and away from drafts, as a sudden chill will cause the leaves to drop off.

When flowering is over, your plant should rest in a cool place. Water it lightly. In April or May the stems should be pruned to about 6 inches and the plant can be repotted outdoors in soil with good drainage. Keep the plant watered well, and in about August pinch off all but the strongest new shoots. Bring your plant inside in the fall, and it should be ready to bloom again for Christmas. The florists also send along this tip: The Poinsettia is a short-day plant and should not receive artificial light after dark.

What can we give to that closest friend or relative who finds it necessary to be far away during the yuletide season? Make him a *Christmas candle* and attach a note which says something like—"Although we are far apart, burn this on Christmas Eve and think of us as we share our Christmas wishes with you."

And, now for the making of those candles. Use an old coffee pot for melting the wax so it will pour slowly and easily through the spout without danger of spilling and burning. You can color your candles by adding oil paint which has been thinned with linseed oil to your wax. A 3-inch squeezing of paint from the tube mixed with a tablespoonful of oil and added to a pint of wax is a good proportion to start. You can then add more coloring, if desired.

Holiday Foods

Sure as Santa Claus has a beard, you are going to want a Christmas cake of some kind included in your holiday menus. *Fruitcake* is usually the leader. Many holiday hostesses use this trick for eliminating wasted slices. When you are serving fruitcake, cut some of the slices large and thin, but also cut cubes and sticks for those who want a smaller portion. These varied shapes make it easy to fashion an attractive dessert platter.

If you have trouble cutting your fruitcake, use your sharpest knife, preferably a serrated one, and use a sawing action. If the cake seems to be a bit sticky and the fruit tends to pull out while cutting, dip your knife in warm water before cutting each slice.

Ever try to garnish *dips* for a holiday party? It can't be done—at least not effectively and permanently—because your lovely garnishes don't last past the first dippers. However, you *can* use ingenuity by inexpensively decorating suitable containers for your dips. Here are a few ideas: Try sticking paper lace, gold braid, ribbon, or other baubles on the outside of the dip dishes. If a stemmed glass compote is to be used, glue the gold braid around the top, and hang tiny gold or colored Christmas balls from the loops in the braid. A pretty perky satin or velvet bow can grace the stem. You will find the tape that is adhesive on both sides does a good job of holding the braids and ribbons in place. These containers can even be carefully washed inside and reused the entire holiday season.

Colored sugar can easily be made for decorating your Christmas sweets by putting a drop or two of food coloring in a jar. Then, pour in a cup of granulated sugar. Cover the jar securely and shake vigorously until the food coloring has completely permeated the sugar. If a deeper color is desired, you can always add more food coloring.

·6·

Beauty Aids that Cost Only Pennies

BEAUTY SALONS are great, but expensive. Here are some ideas on how to care for your hair, nails, and makeup at home, saving time and money.

Hair Care

If you like to wear a *hair net* over your hair at night to save your coiffure—but find your nets are easily torn when put away in the dresser drawer—try this. Take a small plastic medicine bottle, stuff the net into it, and snap on the lid. The hair net will not get torn or lost. A larger bottle can be used for the heavier nets.

If you tease your hair, you will find you always need to "lift" it after each spraying. There is a thing on the market called a *"lift-up comb,"* but if you don't happen to have one, try one of those plastic picnic forks. It works very well!

Summertime can be very hard on your hair. Whether you swim in a pool or an ocean, you will find the chlorine discolors and salt dries your locks. Wear a scarf or hat when sitting in the sun, and rinse the salt or chlorine out of your hair immediately after swimming. There are conditioners on the market which will act as protective shields for hair exposed to sun and surf.

If you *brush* your hair thoroughly before shampooing, you won't have hair in the drain to cause costly plumbing problems.

Now that long hair is back in fashion, here is a tip for those of us who are constantly losing *hairpins*. Bend back one of the ends so it is locked in the hair.

To get a *tight dress* or sweater over your head without disarranging your new hairdo, place a large scarf over your head and hold the four corners of it in your mouth. Pull on the dress, and there will be no muss. It really works.

If you don't have a *shower cap*, use a plastic rain hood. Tie it around your forehead and pull the rest of the cap so that it completely covers your hair, using hair clips to secure it in place.

Here is a trick for making your *hair-do* last a lot longer. How many of us have our hair done beautifully during the day, take every precaution and protective suggestion the beauty operators have to offer for sleeping on the coif without disaster, only to wake up the next morning looking like mother witch looking for her broom? After *years* of being tormented by this, I finally found the answer, which is really very obvious. Spray your hair thoroughly before retiring. Although you may have sprayed it first thing in the morning, there is very little spray left by the end of the day to protect it during the night. Unless you have mastered the art of sleeping on your face, you will find this little "hint" invaluable!

If you don't own a *hair dryer* but are in a rush to set your hair and have it dry, remove the bag from your vacuum cleaner, turn the hose around to "blow," let any remaining dust blow out of it for a minute or so, and proceed to dry your hair with it.

Emergency *hair rollers* can be made from the cardboard tubes that come inside paper towels. Cut them to the desired length and wrap them completely with cellophane wrap or aluminum foil. Punch a few holes to let the air circulate—and you are all set.

Frozen juice cans (with the ends removed and scrubbed out) make great super-size hair rollers. You need only the long clips to secure the hair.

Some housewives who *cut their own hair* tell us they set it in rollers as usual then, when it is dry, they snip the required length off each curl as they take the pins and rollers out. This way, they never lose their place when they get to the back, and they find it is much easier to have each section of hair the exact length they want it.

Do you enjoy *shampooing* your own hair? Well, the experts tell us we should always massage the scalp before a shampoo. Bending over the bathroom sink can really strain the back and arms—especially if you are on the tall side. So, try sudsing your hair in the shower. The constant spray of water will rinse your hair more thoroughly than if you dunk in a sink. If the shampoo you use is still packaged in glass, transfer it to a clean, empty plastic container. Don't risk using a glass bottle in the shower.

Here is another idea for those who like to shampoo in the shower. Place a piece of steel wool over the drain to catch any loose hairs that might stop up the plumbing. (This idea is also good for the utility room tub where you wash your dog.)

Here is a quick way to de-fog that *bathroom mirror* after

a shower. Turn your hand-held hair dryer on it for a few seconds, and it will blow it clear in a jiffy.

Here is a fine substitute for that beauty salon *oil treatment*. Rub baby or cooking oil into your hair before you shampoo. Then cover your oiled locks with plastic wrap and sit under your hair dryer for 15 minutes. The hair dryer will add just the amount of heat needed to make the treatment a success.

How about another idea for giving yourself an inexpensive scalp treatment at home? Apply vegetable oil to your scalp with a piece of cotton. Then, wring a thick Turkish towel out in hot water and secure it around your head. Place the hood of your hair dryer over this, and turn it to medium heat for about 15 minutes. Shampoo your hair in the usual manner.

Wigs and Their Care

Now that more and more women are wearing wigs, some of us find it a problem to keep the *dust* off them when they are stored on head blocks without boxes. Covering the wig with tissue paper or a plastic bag will sometimes flatten the hairdo so that the owner must go through the expense of having it recombed or restyled before wearing it again. Lightly wrapping with tissue isn't too effective because of the many pins it takes to hold the tissue in place. The hairdo is often mangled when the pins are removed. Why not take a plastic rain bonnet and place it loosely over the wig, tying it under the chin of the head block? When you are ready to wear the wig, all you have to do is untie the bonnet strings.

Here is a little trick for making yourself a professional-acting *wig stand* to use when brushing, combing, or styling your wig. Take a plumber's plunger with a long handle— the kind used for stopped-up drains—and attach the plunger to the floor or a table so that it stands perfectly steady. You can then attach a styrofoam head to the handle, and you will have a wig stand that will stay in place during even the most vigorous combings.

When the *foam heads* you use for holding your wigs and hair pieces start chipping away because of pin punctures, here is an easy way to perform an effective repair job. Take masking tape and cross it over the punctured area in a criss-cross fashion. Your head stand will once again hold your hair pieces firmly.

Can't find your *hairnet?* Let your old nylons help you wiggle into your wig. Slip the top of the sock over your head like a stocking cap, and tie a knot at the top of your topknot. Cut off any excess nylon material. Push your hair into the cap, pin it down securely, and you have a dandy, firm foundation on which to place your wig.

Makeup and Skin Care Tips

There is nothing quite like a *facial mask* once a week to tighten and refine your skin. Here is a recipe for a good homemade mask: Mix uncooked oatmeal and water until it is the consistency of paste. Apply to your face and neck and allow it to remain at least 20 minutes. Rinse away with lukewarm water and feel that healthy glow!

Here is another recipe for making your own refreshing facial mask: Use equal parts of Fuller's Earth (purchased at the drug store) and yogurt.

If you have dry skin, you can also make an inexpensive facial mask by peeling and removing the pit from an avocado. Liquefy it in the blender and add 1 tablespoon of honey. Pat on your skin, let dry for 15 to 20 minutes, and rinse off with cool water.

For oily skin, purée a washed, unpeeled cucumber in the blender with 1 tablespoon of plain yogurt. Pat on and let dry for about 20 minutes. Rinse off with cool water.

If wintry weather makes your eyelids look crêpey, gently massage them with a speck of Vaseline and watch them plump up gratefully. The Vaseline can also be used for removing eye makeup.

Many mothers have learned the wonders of inexpensive *baby oil* for removing makeup. It is especially good for use around the sensitive eye area.

What do you do with those old, dried-out *lipsticks?* They can be re-moisturized if you put a thin coating of petroleum jelly all around the lipstick. Give it time to soak in thoroughly before using.

The experts say you will get the most out of your *hand lotion* if you first soak your hands in warm water to open the skin pores. Massage as you work in the lotion.

Here is another use for old *nylon stockings*. Keep one in the bathroom cabinet (tucked into a plastic bag). Whenever you wash or cream your face, tie the stocking, headband fashion, around your head to protect your hair. It can be rinsed out or replaced by the next nylon that develops a run.

No need to buy expensive *lotions*, even if you spend many hours swimming in the pool. You will find that a bit of cream borrowed from the baby is excellent for in-the-pool protection. It rubs in, becoming invisible, and does not readily wash off, because it is especially formulated to offer long-lasting protection for skin subject to excessive moisture.

Pilfer that *salt box* from your kitchen cupboard on your way to your shower. Summer skin flakiness will disappear if you follow Lily Daché's practice of rubbing handfuls of salt all over your body as you stand under the shower. It's great for the circulation, too!

Ever stay in the tub or pool too long and come out as *wrinkled* as a bleached-out prune? Have no fear—rub yourself with a moist salt massage, followed by a light creaming with your favorite lotion.

To get the greatest value out of *bath salts*, softeners, oils, or bubbles, place them in the dry tub directly under the faucet before turning on the hot water.

Out of *bath oil?* Try using baby oil and a splash of your favorite cologne in the bath water.

Keeping your precious *perfume* in a cool, dark place will help prevent evaporation. The stopper should always be replaced securely, and it is wise to retain the box in which it came, to give added protection from light and air.

If you want your perfume to last all evening, apply it right after drying off from a hot bath.

Do you know what to do when the stopper of your favorite bottle of perfume is stuck? Put the bottle into the refrigerator until it is thoroughly cold. You can then remove the stopper with ease. And if you remember to twist the stopper back and forth when you insert it, you can prevent further sticking.

If you have lost a good pair of *earrings* for non-pierced ears lately, you will appreciate this tip. Put a little dab of artificial eyelash adhesive on your ear lobes before donning your earrings. This will keep them where they should be, especially if you go out into cold air and your ear lobes tend to contract.

Beware of putting your *eyebrow pencil* in the pencil sharpener. You will ruin not only the pencil, but the sharpener as well. A sharp knife will do a good job of whittling the end off the eyebrow pencil, and the tip can then be sharpened by rubbing with sandpaper or an emery board.

Thrifty Manicure Tricks

The next time one of those *nail polish bottle* tops insists on sticking, apply a little face cream to the threads on the bottle before closing. It will open easily every time, without breaking the top off the bottle.

If you have an extra toothbrush for your *electric toothbrush* set, you can put it to good use. When you give yourself a manicure, rub the damp brush across the bar of soap, plug it in, and give your nails a really good brushing.

The best time to do a *manicure* is right after washing dishes. This saves the time you would have to spend soaking your cuticles.

To dry *nail polish* quickly, put your hands in cold water when the polish is partly dry, and leave them a couple of minutes. This will make the polish harden.

If you *refrigerate* your nail polish, you will be able to use it up entirely without its getting thick.

Nothing can ruin your manicure quite as fast as the unpleasant job of *scouring*. Here is an idea for conquering the problem—and saving the manicure. Cut your scouring pads in two, and firmly grasp one of the pieces with a snap clothespin. This will enable you to scour away just as effectively, while saving wear and tear on your nails.

The *end papers* left over from home permanents make excellent patches for broken fingernails. Apply a base coat, then cover the break with a bit of the end paper, cut to fit, smoothing it until it adheres firmly. When this is completely dry, apply another coat of the base, and then your coat of fingernail polish.

·7·

Economical Hints
for the Gardener

HERE ARE some ideas to help you with your gardening, indoors or out.

Your Garden Equipment

Are your garden tools getting a bit *rusty*? You can make them shine and last a few more seasons if you apply kerosene to the rusty places and let them stand for a few hours. Rub with a stiff wire brush, and then go over the entire tool with a scouring pad. Rust can be prevented from forming by painting the tools with a good rust-retardant paint.

Automobile paste wax can also prevent your tools from rusting. A light coat of wax will ward off corrosion for quite some time.

Used motor oil also makes a good rust preventive for tools; and it can cost nothing if you change your car's oil and catch the oil you're replacing as it drains off.

Your tools will last a lot longer if they are cleaned and oiled after each use in the garden, and particularly before they are stored away for the winter. Fill a bucket with sand, and pour into this a quart of used crankcase oil. Leave this mixture in the garage or tool shed. Each time you put away a tool, work it around in the oiled sand. The tools will get cleaned and oiled at the same time.

When hanging tools on the garage wall, *outline* them in black paint. You can then tell at a glance what is missing, and borrowers are usually encouraged to put them back.

Strips of *reflector tape*, applied to the handles of your yard and garden tools, will make them easily visible in the dark, protecting them against loss.

Do you have a problem storing your tools with long handles, such as rakes, hoes, spades, etc.? You can make a dandy *portable bin* for these garden tools by adding casters to the bottom of a tall garbage can.

You can make a handy *rack* for your gardening tools if you tack strips of leather to the side of your wheelbarrow to form loops. These loops will hold many of your most often used tools.

A *child's wagon* is a wonderful aid for garden work. You can use it for toting large plastic bags of leaves or other debris, and moving other heavy articles in the garage or basement. It is also a handy container for wheeling your tools easily around with you. A few dollars spent on a wagon will save you time and energy in your gardening, and perhaps keep you from having a backache.

You can put that child's *snow shovel* to good use in summer months by keeping it with your garden tools and using it to pick up grass cuttings and weeds.

When your *ladder* is new, give it a transparent finish of wood preservative or exterior varnish so that the cracks and weak sections will become readily visible, allowing you to reinforce these areas before you have an accident.

When your *trowel* seems too large for digging up seedlings, use your potato peeler. Reach into the soil and lift out the plant roots in the same manner you would use when coring an apple. Transplanting even the smallest seedlings can be expertly done in this manner.

If you find the commercial weeder not doing the "trick" for you, you can *weed* finger-close to your plants if you bend the tines of an old fork at right angles until it assumes a claw shape. Then, sharpen the points on the tines, and you can do a close weeding job without injuring the plants or roots.

You can fashion a *weed puller* in seconds by driving two finishing (small-headed) nails into an old broomstick handle. The heads of the nails, when sunk into the ground and twisted, will pull the weeds out quickly.

That old *bamboo garden rake* can easily be revived by placing the frayed ends into a tub of boiling water. After 10 minutes of soaking, the bamboo will be flexible enough to bend under again with the twist of the wrist and a pair of pliers.

You can easily clean debris and leaves around plants and hedges by using a back scratcher or *toy rake*. This device is especially useful for clearing underneath thorny rose bushes and your more fragile flowers and plants such as moss rose. You will be spared scratches and you will find your job easier.

Do you find gardening hard on your *knees*? Take some old shoulder pads and stitch them inside the knees of your gardening slacks or jeans. You will be surprised how much more comfortable kneeling will be when you are weeding or planting.

Here is an easy way to fertilize the yard without a *spreader*. Punch lots of holes in the bottom of a coffee can, fill the can with fertilizer, replace the lid and shake up and down like a salt shaker. If two or more of these shakers are used simultaneously, the lawn will be fertilized in short order.

Indoor Gardening

To start plants in the house, use eggshell halves filled with loam. Place the shells in the 12 compartments of an egg carton. When the plants are established, transplant them right in the shells. The root formations will break through as the egg shells decompose.

When a *rubber plant* becomes too tall, you can start a new one in the following manner: Make a cut into the stem of the plant about two-thirds of the way through. Keep the cut open by putting a tiny pebble or toothpick in it. Dust with a root-producing hormone, then wrap moist sphagnum moss around the cut, enclosing it in a sheet of thin plastic (like that used in cleaners' bags). Tie the ends to form a moisture-proof pack. When the roots form, cut off below the pack and pot the top plant in soil. New shoots will grow from the old plant. The plant should be kept in a shady, moist place for several weeks.

To keep a cut *rosebud* longer in the bud stage, singe the bottom of the stem with a lighted match just before placing it in water.

Your *cut flowers* will last longer if you mix Sprite or 7-Up with an equal amount of water and add ½ teaspoon of chlorine bleach to each quart of the solution. Flowers absorbing this will stay young longer, say experimenters at Michigan State University.

When you are going away for a week or so, your *bathtub* can become a miniature greenhouse for your small plants. Place them in the tub in saucers so that the bottoms of the pots do not rest in water. Fill the tub with about ¼ inch of water. Open a large plastic cleaner's bag. Poke holes in the plastic, and tape it over the top of the tub. Your plants should survive at least a week.

Or, water your plants thoroughly, wrap polyethylene film around the pot or holder loosely, and you can go off for up to two weeks, knowing your plants are going to survive the neglect. The moisture will be kept in, and light will filter through the plastic. This polyethylene can be purchased at your garden store or nursery.

The greatest *support* you can find for any plant— indoors or out—is a wire coat hanger, which you can easily cut to the desired length. Attach the stalks loosely to the wire with the flexible tie bands that come with plastic bags.

Or, the next time you prune your trees and bushes outdoors, save the sturdier branches to use as indoor stakes. They look more natural than the commercial stakes you buy at the greenhouse or florist, and they cost you nothing.

Do you remember the *eggshell* treatment Grand-mother used to give her house plants? She claimed it was the "secret" of her successful "green thumb," and expert gardeners tell us she might very well have been right. If you put your eggshells into water, let them stand for several hours, and water your plants with this liquid—you, too, will have amazing results. Why? The lime extracted from the eggshells is the "secret."

You can successfully get two plants from one *snake*

plant if you break off the end of one of the stalks and bury it about 2 inches deep in another pot. It will "take"—giving you two plants from one!

Watering your *ferns* once a week with leftover tea provides a tonic which perks them up and promotes growth.

Ferns—which come in a variety of shapes, sizes, and leaf patterns—are beautiful plants to own, but need constant replacing unless we follow precise directions for keeping them beautiful and healthy. Whether you plant yours in the ground or in pots, florists tell us:

Don't move them from place to place. Don't keep them in bright sunlight or where there is a strong wind. Don't handle the tips of the fronds. Don't water them every day—soak thoroughly every third day. Don't remove feelers that grow along the leaves—if your fern is in a pot, wind feelers around so they are out of sight but remain on the plant. Don't keep a fern in a small pot when it has grown large enough to need more soil. Either separate it into two pots or replant the whole fern in a larger pot.

Those wire hangers that come with many hanging plants are ugly—but fancy hangers are quite costly. Decorator's *beads* are very effective solutions. You can cover three or four planter wires with one box of beads. Just string and wind.

Need something to provide proper drainage in those hanging flower pots? Weight counts here—and broken bits of clay pots or rocks leave much to be desired. Why not save nut shells and use them for *drainage?* They do the job just as well, and are very light in weight.

Marbles or fruit pits placed at the bottom of the pot are also good substitutes for clay chips for drainage. They are rounded and serve the purpose of keeping soil in while allowing excess water to drain out.

Save all those worn-out household sponges for use

when potting plants. They also make excellent drainage material and help hold the moisture in the bottom of the pot. Fit pieces of the sponges into the very bottom of the pots and top with soil.

Try planting 8 to 10 orange, lemon, or grapefruit seeds about ½ inch down in the soil of a 4-inch flowerpot. They will produce a lovely *citrus bush* within a year.

You can grow *parsley* in your kitchen all year long. Cut a small, porous sponge in half, place these halves in pretty dishes, and sprinkle a few parsley seeds over the sponges. Keep them moist, and the growing parsley will provide a green plant for your kitchen and a nice garnish for your table.

When transplanting to a *clay pot*, put the pot overnight in water to provide moisture necessary to fill the pores. If you do, the pot won't take moisture from the soil.

Clay flower pots and their matching saucers are attractive, but heed a word of warning. Never put clay pots on a good wood surface unless you have a plate underneath that is not made of clay. Clay containers leak moisture because they are so porous.

One of the most effective and easiest ways to dress up your old clay pots is to decorate them with colored yarns. Spread a bit of glue on the outside of the pot and wind the yarn around it.

Use a bulb-type *baster* to water those popular hanging wall plants, for easy and quick results.

Your house plants should be *watered* with warm tap water that has been standing around for a day or so to reach room temperature. Don't water too often. A plant must dry out before each watering.

Did you know that the glossy-leaved variety of house plant does well with a weekly syringing or *sponging*, while the fuzzy-leaved ones that don't take well to touching by hand should be dusted off with a camel's hair brush? Some plant growers use soapy water to sponge off the foliage of their shiny-leaved plants, but plain water will do the job if all the dust is removed. If the plant is infested with red spider, scale, or other pests, soapy water helps to remove them.

Milk will make the leaves on your house plants shine, but the experts now tell us that the fat in the milk will clog the pores of the leaves.

Ever try using an *envelope moistener* to clean the leaves of your household plants? It works beautifully. This is especially true of the moistener that resembles a tube which you fill with water, which moistens from a small sponge at the end.

What do you use for a *trowel* in your potted plants? A shoe horn is a terrific instrument for this job. Even if the soil has packed down too firmly, your shoe horn will do the necessary spadework with ease. It also reaches deep into the pots to loosen your plants when transplanting.

Do you find a drop or two of water always dribbles onto your tables when watering plants? Wiping the *spills* with a paper towel or cloth usually results in a smear. An ink blotter, however, does a great job. Just place it over the spill and press. It absorbs all the water and leaves no mark. Buy a large one at the stationery store and cut it into convenient pieces.

Before bringing your plants inside for fall and winter, be sure to spray them well to rid them of any *bugs*. If a few eggs should hatch over the winter, take the plants to the open garage and respray.

Outdoor Gardening

Planning to sow a little *grass seed?* Mix a bit of flour with the seed and you can easily see what ground you have already covered.

Or, soak the seed in a laundry bluing–water solution before sowing. Dry, then plant. The birds won't touch it, and germination remains unaffected.

If you see *bald patches* in that new lawn, this time when you reseed shake the seed through a wire kitchen strainer for more even seeding and better results.

Strange as it may seem, new seeds grow well in cool weather, so early spring and fall are the best months to sow new lawns and repair bad spots in old ones.

Cover the newly seeded areas with sheets of *plastic* held in place by stones. This cuts down on the need to sprinkle and keeps the seeds from washing away during a heavy rain. Remove the covering as soon as the seedlings appear.

Looking for *rose bush* protectors? You can easily fashion your own out of one gallon plastic bleach bottles. Cut the tops and bottoms off these plastic containers. Slip the resulting cylinder over the rose bush and fill it with leaves.

When tying your rose bushes together, try using your old nylon stockings. You will find that the thorns catch into the nylon, making it unnecessary to tie the bushes. Twist the stocking loosely, then hook the end to a thorn. The effect will be the same as if you had tied them, yet the soft nylon will never cut into the delicate stems.

Save those gallon *milk cartons*. Cut out the bottom, remove the top lid, and use them to cover your early garden plants.

When it is time to dig up *flower bulbs* and store them for the months when they should "rest," try storing them in egg cartons, labeling the cartons on the outside. This will keep them dry and unbroken until it is time to plant them again.

Those hard-to-hold *vines* can be kept neatly in place by using hair clips which have been sprayed green.

Plastic trellises for plants needn't be costly. Use plastic hangers—the kind that come with some garments but are too flimsy for regular use. Insert one end in the soil, and let the vine climbs on the exposed part. For very large plants, use two or more.

Don't discard that old *sandbox*, even if the children are too old to enjoy it. It makes an excellent place to start seedlings. Add some good rich soil to any remaining sand, and plant. At night, you can cover the box with a discarded plastic shower curtain, securing it with a rock at each corner. This will keep the heat in at night, and the condensation which takes place will keep the seedlings moist. You will be surprised at the way your plantings will thrive in this environment.

You can easily and quickly test old seeds for *germination*. Count out 50 to 100 seeds. Place them between moist newspapers and cover them with a dish. After four or five days examine them to determine the percentage of germination.

Save those lids from *spray cans* (hair spray, deodorant, starch) and use them to start green pepper and tomato plants. Fill them with black soil with a pinch of bone meal. Mix well and water until damp but not soggy. Gently press three or four seeds in each. Cover slightly. Put them near a sunny window, and water and weed as necessary.

Those *plastic bags* which bread comes in are invaluable for holding plants that have been dug up with a ball of soil attached. When transplanting or trading plants with your neighbors, place the plants in these bags and water them. You will find the bag holds the moisture very well. You can tie the bag around the plant loosely, and transplant at your convenience.

Here is an idea for handy and neat *seed storage*. Save your empty match boxes—the kind wooden kitchen matches come in—and glue or tie them together. The front of each box can be labeled with the name of the seeds stored in it, and the "drawers" will pull out easily and separately.

For a quick *cleanup* for gardeners, tie a bag of soap slivers to the outdoor faucet. A mesh onion bag is dandy.

Whether you live in the north or in the south you are likely to start a *fire* in the fireplace during the winter. If so, when the fire is out, sweep the wood ashes into a container that can be stored in a dry, covered place. Wood ashes contain potash and therefore are a fertilizer that is particularly effective for plants like carrots or beets that form thickened rootstocks. As a byproduct of a fire, they cost you nothing.

Don't throw out your old *Christmas tree!* Consider using it for garden mulch. Evergreens are particularly good for azaleas, rhododendrons, and other acid-loving plants.

Simply break off the smaller branches with their needles and spread them around the plant's base. The tree trunk can be burned in the fireplace or made into garden stakes.

Those evergreen boughs from your Christmas tree are also ideal for use as plant protection during cold weather. Spread them over perennials or low plants. They can even shield your taller plants, and make fine wind breakers.

When planting *small seeds* such as carrots or lettuce,

pour them into a small container and add a cup of sand or fine dirt, then mix and plant for easier spacing of plants.

Used *coffee grounds* are worth saving. They are rich in nitrogen and can give a boost to your organic garden, flower bed, or compost pile.

Roses thrive on tea leaves. If you use tea bags, tear them open and collect the used leaves in a container until you have enough to place around the bottom of your rose bushes.

Plastic bags make fine ties to stake up your tomato and pepper plants. Cut 2-inch strips and use them to secure the plant to the stake. The plastic will not cut into the plant.

To keep those *rose beetles* out of your rose garden, plant parsley in your beds. You will have not only healthier roses, but also fresh parsley for cooking.

Plant a row of onions around your garden, or scatter a few mothballs around it, to discourage the *rabbits* from feasting.

If you hesitate to use chemicals in your garden, why not try nature's *bug repellants?* Nasturtiums and rosemary planted in gardens will repel bean beetles, carrot flies, and aphids. If you leave marigolds in over the winter for mulch, they will scare off the round worms and bean beetles. If marigolds are planted around tomato plants, they will keep the bugs away from the tomatoes. Also, if garlic is planted around rose bushes, insects won't bother your pretty roses.

You can also make your own bug control by saving cigar and cigarette butts. Soak them in water for several hours, and sprinkle this solution on rose bushes and other shrubs. It will really control the bugs and aphids.

Are the *birds and squirrels* bothering your garden?

Drive two stakes in the ground—one at either end of the garden. Run a string between them. Then cut cardboard disks from the covers of sour cream and cottage cheese containers. Poke a hole in each disk and suspend a number of them from the string. They twirl in the breeze and keep the birds and squirrels away.

If squirrels raid your bird feeder, and the feeder is mounted on a post, wrap a broad (1 ½-2 feet) piece of sheet metal around the post and nail it in place. Flashing works well. The squirrels don't like to climb the post over the metal.

If you are hounded by *stray dogs* attacking the garbage, sprinkle full-strength ammonia over the bags and the dogs will surely bypass them.

If you are bothered by *ants*, there are several effective remedies for coping with these pesky things without buying commercial ant killers. Here are a few: Dig a hole in the center of the ant hill and insert a quart jar half-filled with detergent water. Place the jar so that the rim is at ground level. You will find that the ants crawl into the jar and drown. You might want to flush out the ants with a hose once in awhile, adding new detergent and water.

Or, pour boiling water into the ant hole. This does the job very effectively—but it sometimes kills the surrounding grass. Some people prefer to make up a bucket of mud, then pour a bit of gasoline into the ant holes. Immediately dump the mud on the ant hole to keep out the air, suffocating the ants.

If the ants are invading your home, sift a small line of red cayenne pepper around the doors and entrances to your house. The ants will not cross through it!

Another good ant-deterrent is to plant mint in the areas where the little pests enter your home. Mint will also serve as a repellant if you place it near your cabbage plants.

Or, place strips of cucumber rind directly across the ants' runway and other places where they are seen. Pouring plain table salt around the area will also discourage large black or small red ants. Some homemakers draw a heavy chalk line across the middle of the threshold. The ants will not cross over this line. Sprinkling ground cloves often does the same trick. What is so unique about all of these ideas? They are *harmless* to pets and small children!

Cut Flowers and Herbs

Have you ever tried picking *fresh lavender* for making your own sachets? The lavender should be picked when the plants are in bud. Both the leaves and the stems are fragrant, but the usual procedure is to remove the leaves and dry them, discarding the stems. When dry, the leaves may be used to stuff small bags made of thin material. These sachets may be used in your bureau drawers and linen closets to remind you all fall and winter of your summer garden.

Did you know that *cut flowers* will last a lot longer and the water will stay fresher if you clip off all the leaves below the water line?

Do you notice that thicker-stemmed blossoms develop unpleasant odors after a day or two in water? This is due to the decay of the stems. The experts tell us that if we place a piece of charcoal in the water, the odor will be considerably improved.

Before arranging the flowers from your garden, condition them so they will last longer. Immerse them in lukewarm water in a cool room for two hours. Then recut the stems with a sharp knife on a bias so they will drink up more water.

You can get that bouquet of mums to last a lot longer if you immerse them in water that has been heated to 100 degrees.

Here is an inexpensive way to *dry flowers*, resulting in

posies that will last for years. Use ten parts of white corn-meal to three parts of borax. Mix it and bury the flowers in it. Let stand for two weeks, and the results will be beautiful!

You can keep your artificial flowers in place with dough-type *wallpaper cleaner*. Put a wad of the cleaner into the vase and arrange your posies. They will really stay just where you want them.

Many a gourmet cook also turns out to be a "gourmet gardener" in an effort to beat the high price of some of the *herbs* that add zest to her cooking. Here are some tips for growing the most often used culinary herbs:

> *Basil* is usually grown in a pot, which makes it a perfect herb to grow indoors during the winter-time. Basil will provide you with fresh leaves for use in soups (especially pea), omelettes, and many Italian dishes.
>
> *Chervil* seeds are slow to germinate, so you may prefer to set out actual plants instead of starting from seeds. Plant them 6 to 8 inches apart, in light shade. Chervil is an annual, and can be used either fresh, dried, or frozen, as a substitute for parsley.
>
> *Coriander* is a hardy annual whose seeds are used for flavoring cookies, gingerbread, sausages, and as a pickling spice. It is also one of the ingredients of curry powder. Coriander seeds should be sown in warm, well-drained soil, covered lightly, and tamped down well. The plants will appear in about two weeks, and approximately 90 days after sowing, brown seeds will appear. These are cracked open and the inside kernels are used in cooking after they have been dried in the sun for two or three days.
>
> *Dill* seeds should be sown barely covered with soil (or set out dill plants). Dill is an annual, with seeds

germinating in about a week. The plants will grow 2 or 3 feet tall, and can be used either fresh or dried when cooking fish or potatoes, or for pickling cucumbers.

Fennel should be sown in well-drained soil and full sunlight. It is an annual. The seeds will germinate in a week to 10 days, and should be thinned to about 10 inches apart. This herb has a delicate licorice flavor and is used in breads and rolls, or sprinkled on potatoes, salads, and seafood dishes.

Chives, unlike many herbs, prefer a fairly rich soil. They can be grown indoors in pots, and should be fed with liquid fertilizer once a month. Chives are used for a delicate onion flavor.

Mint likes moderately rich, moist soil. The flower buds should be picked in order to preserve the fine mint flavor of the leaves. The problem is not in growing mint, but in confining it. It spreads rapidly, and there are 14 varieties of mint—all of which are used for jellies, sauces, juleps, and tea.

Sage is easy to grow. The seeds should be sown about 2 feet apart. Two-year-old plants can be divided to make new clumps. Leaves should be cut for drying in the fall, but don't strip the plant completely of foliage. The dried leaves are used in poultry dressings, or tea.

Oregano can be grown from seed, or set out plants. Scatter the seeds on top of the ground, covering lightly with soil. Young plants should be placed a foot apart in full sun. Oregano is used in salads, pizzas, meatballs, and Italian dishes.

Sweet Marjoram is an annual which can be started from seeds, or set plants out about a foot apart. It is used in many recipes for roast lamb and baked fish, and is excellent in salads and egg dishes.

Rosemary should be set in full sun and fertile soil. It will make an attractive, low hedge in the garden, but it should be taken in and potted before the ground freezes in the fall. It is a delightful addition to roast pork, chicken, or lamb.

Tarragon is a hardy perennial whose leaves can be used either dried or fresh. Tarragon plants need rich, sandy loam and should be set in full sunlight about 18 inches apart. Tarragon gives vinegar a mild licorice flavor, and is tasty on steaks, chops, lobster, and roast beef, or in fish sauces.

Thyme, when grown in its native Greece, is planted on dry, rocky hillsides, benefiting from spring torrents. It requires good, fast drainage and limy soil. Mulch thyme in late fall with a mixture of sand, compost, and bone meal. This herb is perfect with meats or when used in clam chowder.

When it is time to bring your herbs inside for winter use, spread them on cheesecloth or screening in a dark, well-ventilated place for a week. When they become brittle, strip the leaves and store them in airtight jars in a dark place. For cooking, crush about a third as much as you would use of fresh herbs.

·8·

Thrifty Gifts and Wrappings

HERE ARE some ideas on how to prepare and wrap beautiful gifts, inexpensively, as well as some tips on mailing.

Gift Ideas

What do you do with those old *TV dinner trays?* These can be made into dandy gifts for shut-ins or people in convalescent homes. Girl Scout groups put different fruits in the various sections, tucking in packages of foil-wrapped fudge. They then cover it all with clear plastic wrap, tie with a ribbon and slip in a cheery note or card.

Husbands also enjoy using these trays in the workshop for holding the parts of an object they may be repairing. In this way, the parts are never mixed with other things on the workbench.

Or, give them to the gal who enjoys dabbling in art work. They are excellent for stacking near paint supplies, because a different tray can be used for each medium in which the artist is working. The trays can be discarded after the picture has been completed.

Here is an idea for a *gift container* when you wish to surprise a friend or neighbor with two or three long-stemmed roses. Use those tall Alka-Seltzer bottles or the tall, narrow olive bottles. They can be sprayed with colored gilt. A ribbon at the top of the bottle will hide the glass screw threads, giving it a "gift-like" touch.

A half-pound *coffee can* becomes an attractive gift for any occasion when lined inside and out with aluminum foil and filled with homemade candies, cookies, or other goodies. Decorate the plastic top with a paper doily cut to size and topped with a pretty ribbon pompom. You can enhance this gift by unrolling one of those all-purpose scouring pads (they come in quite a few lovely colors). Slip it over the can, and roll it a bit on the top and the bottom. When the goodies are gone, the scouring pad can be removed and used by the recipient.

Here is a dandy job for a grade-school child who is looking for something to do on a rainy day. Buy a supply of skimpy ten-cent *potholders* from the dime store and let her sew two together with strong thread. In just a few minutes she can create a thick, safe and handy potholder for mother, or to give to grandmother as a gift. Many of the quilted potholders sold today are really too thin to be safe for handling heavy, hot roasting pans. The crocheted "bazaar" types have too much openwork to be practical. Even the handwoven squares are usually too small and too thin for adequate protection. So, let your child make a really useful kitchen item. This could be an excellent time to teach her the art of blanket stitching, which will make a lovely edging for those potholders.

In the fall you find many drug stores and department

stores selling plastic foam *ice buckets* for about 39 cents. Buy a few and use them for mailing your Christmas cookies to relatives and friends. The cookies will arrive in perfect condition and the ice buckets weigh so little that the postage is not exorbitant.

Do you ever run short of time and money around the holidays? How about writing some *"gift-for-the-future"* notes: a few hours of babysitting for a friend with small children, a promise to care for pets or plants for a traveling friend, a dinner at a super restaurant for someone you would like to dine with, a promise to make needlepoint covers for dad's golf club heads, or a needlepoint cover for mom's tennis racquet. Or, present a gift of lessons to a friend if you happen to be proficient at sewing, needlepoint, chess, backgammon, etc.

If your family is going to spend some time visiting another house this Christmas, and you want to bring them something more durable than candy, how about a *family game?* "Perfection" intrigues people of all ages. Or, what about a Ouija board? "Monopoly" is available for as little as $5, or you can get a deluxe version with extras such as wooden houses and hotels and gold-toned tokens. "Scrabble" is another fun game for all ages that now comes in a deluxe version with letter bag and turntable.

Baby food containers make marvelous gift jars for your homemade jelly and jams. Sterilize before filling and cover with a thin layer of paraffin.

Purchase a set of felt markers especially designed to use on fabric, and you can create many attractive *T-shirts* with them. However, be sure the markers you buy are the permanent kind. This is a great way to teach children to make gifts for their friends. Grandparents would love pillow cases or kitchen towels decorated with the markers by their grandchildren.

When gift-buying time comes, some of us don't exactly know what to give. If the recipient wants to exchange the gift, he has to have a *receipt*; but, no giver wants to let on how much he paid for the gift. What can you do? Here's the answer:

When buying the gift, ask the clerk to give you two receipts; one for you with the price and the other one with the description of the item and everything but the price. Enclose this one with the gift, and the recipient can exchange the item without any trouble.

When children receive gifts from *out of town*, have a picture taken of them playing with it or using it to send to the donor in the thank-you note

Here is a dandy idea for a *baby shower* gift. Give a diaper bag or plastic baby tub, filled with useful items such as washcloths, baby shampoo, powder, soap, etc. If the shower is given after the baby arrives, you might even include cans of prescribed formula.

Looking for a unique, inexpensive gift to bring to a friend who is hospitalized? Make a get-well *grab bag*. Using a straw tote bag, or any decorative shopping bag— individually wrap little gifts such as a scratch pad with a ballpoint pen taped to it, a box of note cards, the latest issue of your favorite magazine, a deck of cards, even a box of homemade cookies or candies. This is sure to be a conversation piece not easily forgotten.

Shower Presents

Any month today can be "Bridal Shower Month," and here are some ideas for gifts that will be easy on the budget as well as time-savers for the bride-to-be:

Why not wrap those shower gifts in colorful *kitchen*

towels instead of paper? The recipient will appreciate your originality.

Looking for a unique gift? Why not fashion a *"medicine chest"*? A rectangular box can be covered with white paper to resemble a medicine cabinet and a piece of aluminum foil can be glued to the front so it looks like a mirror. Inside the box you can place the things usually found in a medicine cabinet—toothpaste, toothbrushes, hair spray, deodorant, mouthwash, bandaids, etc. Just another area in which you can save a considerable amount of money for the young couple soon to set up housekeeping.

Another shower gift idea is to give a large *spaghetti kettle*—the kind that can also be used for corn on the cob, soups, etc. In the kettle you can put your favorite spaghetti sauce recipe, a package of spaghetti, a container of grated Italian cheese, a package of bread sticks, salad dressing, and perhaps a bottle of Chianti. The makings for the very first dinner in the couple's new home will be there.

I have always said, "If I had to choose one last meal I would choose an Italian spaghetti dinner . . . but the recipe for the sauce and meatballs would have to be my own." I am going to share it with you, and perhaps you can share it with a new bride. This recipe makes about ten generous servings, and can be frozen in plastic containers for a quick meal on a busy day:

Spaghetti & Meatball Sauce À La Laird

6 lbs. ground chuck	3 large cans tomato purée
2 pkg. dry onion soup	3 large cans peeled tomatoes
2 T salt	2 T pepper
2 T garlic powder	2 T oregano
2 eggs	1 C cornflake crumbs
	2 T parsley flakes

Divide ground chuck in half. Brown 3 pounds in a heavy, large kettle. Add one package dry onion soup, tomato purée, tomatoes, salt, pepper, garlic powder, and oregano to taste. Simmer sauce ½ hour. While sauce is cooking, mix in a large bowl 3 pounds ground chuck with 1 pkg. dry onion soup, salt, pepper, garlic powder, and parsley flakes to taste (approx. 1 tsp. of each), 2 eggs, 1 cup corn flake crumbs. Form into meat balls. Turn up the heat under the sauce so it reaches a rolling boil. Drop the meatballs into boiling sauce. (This is an old Italian "secret" to keep meatballs from falling apart.) Simmer the sauce and meatballs for a minimum of 2 hours. (The longer it is simmered, the thicker it gets.) Serve over No. 9 spaghetti or Vermicelli which has been cooked according to directions. Tossed green salad and garlic bread will complete your gourmet Italian meal.

Another idea for that bridal shower: Have each guest bring her favorite *recipe*, along with a utensil for the dish. (The hostess might provide the bride with a recipe file box.) For example: A banana nut bread recipe with loaf pan, a recipe for western-fried potatoes and a skillet, an omelet recipe with an omelet pan, lasagna recipe with lasagna pan, crêpes cookbook with a crêpe pan, etc.

Wrap those bridal shower gifts in *handi-wipes*, and decorate the package with copper scouring pads or plastic measuring spoons. It will make a pretty package, and there is no waste. The bride can make good use of her "wrappings."

Or, give that bride-to-be a set of *tools*—a hammer, screwdriver, and pliers for her own use. Many young brides are do-it-yourselfers these days.

For a really unique shower gift, give the bride-to-be the ingredients to make her first *loaf of bread*—a bread pan, rolling pin, and the dough (U.S. currency). Wrap the currency around the rolling pin and enclose in see-through plastic wrap. You might include the inscription, "Here is a little dough to make your first loaf of bread"—along with your favorite bread recipe.

A very thoughtful gift for a bride from a relative of the groom is an *address book* in which are listed the names, addresses, and telephone numbers of her future relatives, including aunts, uncles, and cousins as well as the immediate family. It will be a great help to her because often the groom does not keep this kind of record.

Wrapping Ideas

You can restore wrapping paper for use once again by turning it on the wrong side, sprinkling lightly with spray starch, and *ironing* with a warm iron. The gift wrap will come out as crisp and smooth as new.

Do you enjoy doing your own gift wrapping? The next time you wrap a gift for a *bridal shower* why not arrange the ribbons in narrow strips going both ways on top of the package to make checks about 3 or 4 inches wide. Into these vacant spaces you can paste your favorite recipes. The bride is sure to be delighted, your gift-wrapping idea will be quite a conversation piece!

Which is the best buy—flat sheets or rolls of gift *wrapping papers?* According to the *Co-Op Consumer*, flat sheets are much cheaper. At this writing, for instance, you can buy 72 square feet of flat sheets for about 83 cents. Compare that to the $1.38 for a roll containing 60 square feet.

Wrap the kids' Christmas presents in the *color comics* from the paper. They'll be intrigued and you'll save a good deal on wrapping paper.

Why not gift wrap your *Christmas packages* as you purchase them—instead of waiting until the job becomes a gigantic task? You will actually enjoy wrapping just a few packages at a time—and the results will look a lot better. Also, early wrapping of your gifts means that you will be buying the gift wrap before the rush, when more items are available.

Here is the answer to wrapping *bulky gifts* that are too big for wrapping paper. Buy brightly colored shelf paper (it comes in two widths)—and trim with colored ribbons. You will find this much less expensive than even the continuous-roll gift wrap.

A roll of inexpensive wallpaper also makes a wonderful gift wrap for games and other large gifts.

Save those empty cartons in which a jumbo-size roll of *tin foil* is packed and use it to hold the spools of gift ribbon when you are doing your Christmas gift wrapping. Stand the spools vertically in the carton side by side. Cut slits in the carton top, one for each spool, and pull the ribbons through. No more ribbon spools rolling off the table and onto the floor.

Mother can get cooperation from almost every member of her family when it comes to neatly *unwrapping* the birthday or Christmas gifts, if she offers a prize for doing a good job. This little extra "gift" should be purchased ahead of time—and be appropriate for any age or sex. Carefully folding the pretty paper and ribbon, which can be reconditioned and reused next year, will save considerably on the cost of the following year's wrappings.

Here is another idea for those of you who would like your gift wrappings to retain their beauty after the package has been opened. Try wrapping the top and bottom of the gift box separately. The recipient has only to remove the cover instead of the paper.

You can easily solve the problem of having to *open for inspection* (and ruin the wrappings of) gift packages that you take on planes. Wrap the lids and the boxes separately, attaching a single bow to the lid. You can then remove the lid for inspection at the airport. (Use rubber bands to hold the lids of the gifts on.)

If you really want to make gift wrapping easy, purchase one of the large office-size dispensers for *transparent tape* available at all stationery stores. It is heavy enough so you can tear off the tape with one hand while holding the wrapping paper in place with the other. And, it's big enough not to get misplaced between package-wrapping sessions. This is the economical way of doing it too, when you stop to consider how many little containers of tape one buys each year.

When wrapping gifts, why not put your *lazy susan* to good use? It can hold all the necessary accessories—such as ribbons, seals, pen, tape, glue, scissors, etc. It will require only a flick of the finger to reach the necessary equipment.

Trim your gift packages with *glitter* from the variety store. Dab a bit of paste onto the bows of your packages and sprinkle them with glitter for a lovely effect.

Don't throw away those strips of *nylon net* left from your sewing projects. Put them away carefully and use them for tying gifts. It saves buying ribbons, and they make lovely ties and bows.

Mailing

When mailing those Christmas packages, you can make a *shockproof wrap* against rough handling if you line the inside of a firm packing box with empty egg cartons. Surround the gifts generously with crumpled paper so the cartons won't shift in the box—and there you are!

Here is another handy hint for anyone who has to send gifts through the mail. How many times have you found that the *outer wrappings* have become damp due to inclement weather, or perhaps the package has been left on the doorstep because the addressee is not at home at the time of delivery? Gift wrap your package as usual, then slip it into a plastic bag (the kind clothes come back from the cleaners in will usually do nicely). Then, put the outer wrapping on the package. The gift, thus protected, will not get damp even if the outer coverings are thoroughly soaked. Smaller packages can even be wrapped in plastic bread wrappers for protection.

Ever pack gifts for mailing, but wonder how to protect that frilly bow you have worked so diligently to make extra-lovely? Take one of those plastic *berry baskets* and cover the bow with it. You will find it light enough to make the outer wrapping easy, yet it has enough strength to guard the bow from crushing.

Whenever you find it necessary to mail packages to members of your family, why not make every inch of space "count"? Many of us hate to pay postage for the crumpled or shredded paper used to fill in the spaces. Why not fill those empty spaces with *sponges*, instead? They can be purchased in a variety of sizes and colors, are not heavy, provide the perfect cushioning for the contents of the box, and will be most useful to the recipient.

When getting out-of-town gifts wrapped and ready for mailing, make a more secure wrap by *wetting the string* before tying. As it dries, it will shrink and make a firmer knot.

Be sure that the *boxes* you use are very sturdy. If the gift comes from the store in a flimsy box, enclose it in a stronger one. Those brown paper grocery bags, cut open, make good outer wrap. Be sure to use both tape and twine to secure each package.

Place your *return address* on a card inside the package as well as on the outside. Should the address be obliterated, the package will be returned to you and will not end up at the dead-letter office.

Ripped-up newspaper or popcorn makes a dandy *filler* for large boxes. And, for mailing breakable objects, the protective plastic wrap used by many department stores, called "Bubble-Pak," is now available to the consumer.

When sending a *coin* through the mail, clip the corner from a used envelope, insert the coin, and tape the open side closed as you attach it to the letter. This eliminates the shifting and possible loss of the coin.

Or, make a pocket for the coin out of gummed photograph mounts. All you will need will be two corners to keep the coin neatly and securely in place.

When *stamps* get wet and stick together, you needn't throw them away. Place them in a shallow dish filled with water, let them soak a bit, and then pull them apart gently under slowly running water. Place them face down on paper toweling to dry, then glue them into your stamp book or onto your envelopes.

Here is another idea for those stuck-together stamps. Try running a hot iron over them, then separating them quickly before the glue has a chance to cool again.

You can detach a stamp—intact—from an envelope, by using a drop of *lighter fluid*.

Here is a dandy way to remove an unused *stamp* from one envelope and transfer it to another without having to iron it or steam it. Tear the envelope around the stamp, leaving about a ¼-inch paper border. Then place the stamp on a wet surface such as a damp sponge, with the paper side down. Allow it to remain there a few minutes until the moisture soaks through the paper. The stamp will lift right off with enough glue remaining on it so that it can be placed on another envelope immediately.

Here is an idea to use when you must enclose a stamp, or stamps, in a letter or order and wonder how to attach the stamp so that it won't get lost when the envelope is opened. When buying stamps, get some just for this purpose by specifying that you want an outside row of a *commemorative stamp*. Attached to the stamp, but perforated at the edge, is a length of preglued paper which is all you will dampen. Stick that tab to the letter. The receiver will tear at the perforation line and have a clean, fresh stamp.

When sending *stamps* through the mail, dust the backs with a sprinkle of talcum powder so that they won't stick together.

Unused *envelopes* which have sealed themselves due to moisture in the air, needn't be discarded. Put them in your freezer. In a half hour or so, they will unstick so that you can pull them apart easily without damaging the glue.

If the adhesive on an *envelope flap* won't stick, don't pitch it. Try a quick application of clear nail polish. It dries quickly, leaves no smudge, and can't ever be steamed open.

Quite often, manufacturers offer cash or *prizes* in exchange for a label that must be removed from a bottle. However, they seldom tell you how to remove the label. Don't bother struggling with a knife, scissors, or a razor blade. Stand the empty bottle upside down in a mug of warm water overnight. The label will slip off in the morning—intact.

When sending in *box tops* or other proofs of purchase from cardboard boxes, remove as much of the backing as possible. With the high cost of postage these days, extra backing could be costly, especially if the offer requires more than one box top.

If you are out of *postcards* (and the contest directions specify *only* postcards), you can "make" your own. Seal a plain envelope and write the message on the back. Stamp and address the front. The same method can be used when the directions say: "Attach your entry to a post card." In this case, you would seal the flap and glue or scotch tape your entry to the back of the envelope, leaving the front of the envelope for the address. Chances are both methods will qualify. Even though the instructions specify "postcards," the reason they do is that the manufacturer doesn't want his personnel to have to go through the time and trouble of opening envelopes.

Use a piece of carbon paper and a second sheet when ordering from *catalogs*. Place the carbon and second sheet underneath the order blank. Then you will have a complete record of what was ordered, and when you ordered it. If the item is lost or delayed, you will have an exact copy.

·9·

Don't Pitch It—
Fix It

HERE IS an alphabetical listing of many jobs that you can do yourself, to save expensive repairs or replacement costs.

Here is an idea for keeping those rolls of *adhesive tape* and gummed tape dry and usable for a long time, even in the most humid climate: Store them in covered glass jars, and they will be dry and usable indefinitely.

Don't discard those *artificial flowers* because they are dust catchers and hard to keep clean. You can make them garden fresh again by popping them into a paper bag to which you have added a cup of corn meal. Shake them, and the dust will disappear.

The ink in some *ballpoint pens* tends to dry, especially if they are not used frequently. The ink also tends to thicken in cold weather. Stick most of the pen under the water faucet for a few minutes and run hot water over it, then dry with paper toweling. This usually solves the problem and starts the ink flowing freely again.

Or, if your ballpoint pen won't write and you know it's not out of ink, lightly rub a pencil eraser across the paper where you plan to write, and the pen will write easily.

If your *bathroom scale* has become rusty or dingy-looking with age, it can be easily covered with adhesive-backed paper. Cut with a safety razor blade for a neat job. The scale will be new-looking again, as well as quite waterproof. If you cover the bottom with the paper also, you will prevent those rust marks that sometimes mar the bathroom floor.

When your favorite *bedspread* shows signs of the threads breaking, extend its life expectancy by machine-stitching a single bed sheet to the underside. This will supply the needed strength, while being inconspicuous.

You can easily loosen tight *bolts* and screws by using a few drops of hydrogen peroxide. Let it soak for a while. If the bolts or screws have rusted, try using a little penetrating oil along with the peroxide.

There are several simple and inexpensive ways to clean an old *brass bed*, making it look like new. One is to apply tomato catsup with a cloth! Let it stand a few seconds, then wipe off and polish. Do just a small section at a time, for a beautiful polishing job.

Or, make a paste from wood ashes (from the fireplace) and lemon juice. Apply with a cloth and polish with a flannel cloth or chamois.

Remember that new brass beds usually have a lacquer on them, and polishing will remove this, oftentimes in an uneven manner. Old brass beds which have not been lacquered will stay polished and untarnished for quite some time with either of these homemade polishes.

If those *brass headboards* rub against the wall, chipping the paint and making a redecorating job necessary quite often, here is a dandy remedy. Drill holes on the lower portion of the headboard, one on each side. Insert long screws with 2-inch heads through the holes you have drilled, securing them with bolts. Now here's the trick: Take two small rubber doorstop caps (which can be bought at any dime store or hardware store), and fit them tightly over the screw heads. These will keep the headboard away from the wall, and should a child happen to bounce on the bed and the rubber-capped screw hit the painted surface, no damage will be done. This works equally well for a heavy chair or sofa which knocks against a wall.

An old *broom* with frayed and spreading bristles can be renewed if you soak the bristles in water for a few minutes, then snap a couple of heavy rubber bands around them below the stitching. After the bristles dry, remove the rubber bands.

You can increase the usefulness of your old *brushes* with lacquer. Apply lacquer at the base of the brush to prevent the bristles shedding, giving you much more use out of this item.

Don't pitch those *bunk beds* because small toddlers are apt to fall from the top bunk—make trundle beds out of them. If the bunk beds have two high headboards, use one as the head and one as the foot of the top bed. Use the two low footboards at either end of the low bed and slide it under the higher one. Casters can be added to make it easier to slide the lower bed in and out.

You may also find the upper bed should be raised a bit so that the other bed will slide under it. If so, use wooden blocks about 8 inches long and 3 inches thick to build up the upper bed so the headboard on the low bed will clear its underside.

Instead of whittling a *candle* at the base to make it fit the holder, hold the end of the candle in a cup of hot water for a few minutes. It will soften enough to be pressed firmly into the holder.

How can you prevent mildew from forming on *canvas awnings*, canvas boat covers, etc.? Try sprinkling salt on them as you roll them up. The salt will absorb any moisture that may have been left on the canvas, leaving the surface dry. This also works effectively on camping tents which are stored from vacation to vacation.

A solution of camphor will do a good job of cleaning soiled *playing cards*. Only a small amount of camphor is needed—and a light, quick touch of the hand.

When your playing cards begin to stick together, just put them into a paper bag, sift a little talcum powder on them, and shake the bag. They will not only slide easily, but will smell fresh, too.

Give a new lift to that old *card table*. Wallpaper the top, and apply two thin coats of shellac. A good waxing, after the shellac, completes the job.

If your *cedar chest* has lost its scent, sand the interior lightly with fine-grained sandpaper.

Here is an easy way to repair a link which has spread apart in a small *chain necklace*. Insert a toothpick in the two adjacent links to hold the faulty link in place, then pinch it together with pliers.

Cut the time spent trying to untangle a fine chain necklace this easy way. Place a few drops of salad oil on a piece of waxed paper. Lay the knot in the oil and pick at it with two pins until it "slides" apart.

Ever try using modeling clay to hold together pieces of your good *china* or glass that you are mending? It does a dandy job of holding the pieces together until the glue is dry. The clay can be easily wiped off later.

You can improve the appearance of *cracked china* by boiling it in milk for about 45 minutes.

Don't pitch those old *clay pots*. Cover them with foil to make beautiful containers for your indoor house plants.

Instead of discarding a cracked flower pot, make it useful again by holding it together with a wide band of rubber cut from an old inner tube. Stretch a section of the tube up over the base of the pot. You can paint it to match, if you so desire.

Clothespins which have been left out in the rain will make black marks on your clothes—unless you do the following: Soak the clothespins in equal parts of liquid bleach and water for about an hour. Rinse them thoroughly and dry them on cake racks in the sun. The rinsing process is most important so they don't leave bleach spots on your colored clothes.

Make *cushion covers* out of old, lined draperies that are too good to throw away. This is quick and easy, because the cushion can be inserted between the drapery and the lining. Sew up the other sides and you will have dandy cushions for the children to sit on while watching television.

If you have a *door* that keeps slamming in the breeze, wedge a soft nylon sponge under it. There will be no doorstop to trip over.

When doors that squeak in the night disturb your sleep, you can bet the problem lies with the hinges. There is a lubricant in a spray can, called WD-40 sold in hardware stores and lumber yards. Just a quick spray will silence that squeaky hinge.

A slit powder puff, put over the *doorknob*, keeps it from marking the walls when doors are opened too wide. It also serves as a bumper and eliminates noise.

Plagued by loose knobs or other fixtures that won't stay

in place? Partially unscrew them and wind the screw with thread. Then screw tightly back into place.

Did you know that sun and heat pouring through lightweight *draperies* or curtains, especially picture windows or "walls of glass" can add 5 degrees of warmth to any room? Any window that gets sun should have lined curtains or draperies in summer. An inexpensive way to do this is to use a plastic lining, hanging it with the draperies on the hooks you already have. This lining is available in any good drapery department.

If your *cafe curtain rings* bind when pulled across the drapery rod, put some spray wax on a cloth and wipe the rods with the wax. The draperies will then glide across with just a slight touch.

When you take those draperies down to send to the cleaners, remove the *drapery pins* and mark each place where a pin has been with a marking pen. When the draperies return from the cleaners, the marks will still be obvious. In go the pins in the proper places, in a jiffy.

Sticky *drawers* should never be forced open! Try rubbing the sticking surface with paraffin, an old candle, or hard laundry soap. If this doesn't do the trick, perhaps you had better sand the edges down a little bit.

When an item with moving parts, such as a large circulating *fan*, the fan on your furnace, or even a ceiling fan in the bathroom becomes a bit too noisy for comfort, chances are it only needs a bit of penetrating oil. This can be a real problem if you can't reach the oil holes with your oil can, or if the item cannot easily be taken apart for oiling. Try putting a piece of cotton batting on the end of a knitting needle, or drop a few drops of the penetrating oil into the slotted end of a long Phillips screwdriver. Insert this apparatus into the area to be oiled, and you can look forward to having a quiet, noise-free appliance once again.

Do you have a rusty *fireplace screen?* Use a rust-removal lubricant. Then wire-brush the screen to remove all soil and dirt. Spray with heat-resistant metal enamel. Your screen will look like new!

Is a squeaky *floor* driving you up the wall? You can easily fix it. First, find which floor boards are rubbing together. (That's what causes the squeak.) Then squeeze powdered graphite, talcum powder, or liquid soap into the crack between the boards. Use a putty knife, and push the lubricant down.

There are several ways you can inexpensively fix floor cracks. One is to buy a can of wood crack filler at a building supply store. Use as a paste as it comes out of the can. When it is dry, sand the area.

Or, get some fine sawdust from the same type of wood and mix it with all-purpose white glue to form a paste. Fill the cracks with this paste and allow it to dry. Sand and varnish.

You can also make your own crack filler for wood by mixing some flour with enough shellac to make a paste. Rub this filler on the wood, and after it has dried completely, sandpaper the surface and rub with a soft cloth and thin shellac.

Furniture Repair

If your varnished or shellacked furniture has *white spots* or rings on it, you can effectively restore the original finish. Dampen a cloth with spirits of camphor or essence of peppermint and dab it on the spot. Do not wipe, but let dry undisturbed for at least 30 minutes. Then, rub down with rottenstone and oil and the white spots will disappear. (This method does not work well on lacquered finishes, only those which have been varnished or shellacked.)

When driving a *small nail* or furniture tack, use a piece of cardboard, such as a portion of a matchbook cover.

Push the nail through the cardboard and position it. You won't hit your fingers, and you will find this works even better than a magnetized hammer.

Seats and backs for *canvas furniture* (or cotton duck) are easily replaced in the following manner: Used the original seat or back for a pattern, allowing a few inches for stretching. (Remember, this is why they have to be replaced—they stretched beyond the point of staying together.) Metal furniture can usually be taken apart to slip the old seats and backs off and your brand new replacements on. Furniture made of wood usually sports fasteners that can be removed. If the canvas or duck was originally tacked onto the frame, secure your replacement pieces with tacks. If loops were sewn in and slipped over rungs, do the same with yours. When stitching your seams, be sure to double back and sew a second seam for greater strength.

There are times when a slit, tear, or hole can be effectively patched instead of replacing the whole area. When this is the case, feather the edges of the hole by removing a few of the threads parallel to the opening. Cut a patch of the same material and cement it behind the tear with fabric-mending cement.

It might be well to remember that ready-made replacements can usually be bought for yacht, director, circle, butterfly, and sling chairs, chaises, or cots. You have only to slip them onto the frames over the dowels or metal tubes.

If your problem happens to be faded or worn canvas seats and backs, you might be able to brighten them by painting or treating them with a fabric spray. Two coats are usually needed over stripes and plaids, but one coat will cover solid colors.

If the wooden surfaces are scratched and nicked, try shoe polish. It is very effective when applied with a cotton-tipped toothpick. Rub carefully over the blemish, then buff dry. If the color turns out darker than your wood tone, the polish can be erased with naptha. The polish will shine when it is buffed, so if the furniture has a dull finish, be careful not to buff.

If your furniture is red-finished *mahogany* and you have a few scratches on it, try new iodine. For brown or cherry-colored mahogany, iodine which has turned brown with age will do a good job. If your furniture is maple, dilute iodine about 50 percent with denatured alcohol to give it the right color to blend perfectly.

For *dents* in solid wood furniture, one refinisher prescribes filling an eyedropper with water and dripping water into the dent every day or so. The dent will disappear as the wood absorbs the water and expands.

Rattan furniture, with its many rounded, curved pieces and wrapped joints, takes a great deal of time and patience to refinish. However, the end results are usually more than worth the effort. The experts tell us that if the original finish is shellac, it should be removed with a brush followed by a cloth soaked in alcohol or shellac thinner. If the old finish is paint or varnish, brush on a water-rinse paint remover. Using a small brush, brush out the joints, then rinse. Sand the larger areas until they are smooth, using a dull-tipped knife to clean out the crevices. Each nail must be treated with a clear, rust-proofing sealer. Joints that have broken or worked loose can be repaired by soaking the bamboo bindings in water until they will bend like a cord. Apply waterproof glue to the broken joints. Tack one end of binding, wrap as tightly as possible, then fasten the end with a zinc-coated nail or brad.

If you would like to replace the torn, frayed, worn, and stretched seats and backs of your *summer furniture* with bright, new plastic webbing, here is how: On wood furniture, tack the webbing to the frames with nonrusting tacks, wrapping the webbing around each rung and using at least three tacks.

On steel or aluminum frames, fold the webbing ends into two triangles, providing at least four layers and a single point for fastening. The ends of the webbing can be most effectively attached with a washer under a tapping screw.

Stop that metal *patio furniture* from rusting by giving it a coat of liquid car wax.

The experts tell us that good wooden summer furniture can be rebuilt and refined to last for years. For example, triangular blocks can be successfully glued into the corners of wobbly seat frames to make them sturdy once again. If rungs or legs are loose, remove them, clean off all the glue, then re-insert the legs with fresh glue. Cracked or broken rungs can be re-glued and wrapped tightly with cord over wax paper until the cord sets. The type of glue used for rebuilding outdoor furniture should always be 100 percent waterproof.

You will find that redwood and cedar chairs, tables, and picnic sets dent and scratch easily, as they are made from soft woods. A water-rinse paint remover will quickly loosen cracked or peeling coats of varnish. Rinse with clear water and allow to dry thoroughly. Surface stains and marks can then be removed with fine sandpaper. Be careful of splinters, especially when rounding the edges and corners. You can then finish the redwood and cedar in their natural color without varnish by applying several layers of a clear or lightly tinted wood stain. Be sure to apply these wood penetrating finishes only when the furniture is thoroughly dry, so that the porous wood will soak up the finish satisfactorily.

If you prefer to have a hard, clear coating that will prevent grease or other stains from soaking in, apply at least three coats of marine varnish to the bare wood with no sealer or undercoating.

For minor repairs to woven straw summer furniture, cut strips from a plastic container, such as a bleach bottle, and weave the strips into the straw to cover the holes. A paint job will cover the patches.

Wicker outdoor furniture was made to last forever. But what happens when the inevitable occurs . . . it needs refinishing? If the old finish is badly deteriorated, brush on a heavy water-rinse paint remove. Let it remain on the furniture for at least an hour, then brush the surface with a stiff brush, hosing off the residue.

When the wicker is dry, rub the surfaces with a large wad of steel wool. Any broken pieces should be replaced with pieces of the same size, stained to match the others. Apply two coats of varnish, or a combination of varnish and stain. (Since wicker furniture is somewhat less than a picnic to refinish, take extra good care of it and avoid unnecessary exposure to weather.)

When those old-fashioned *cane chair seats* become soiled, they needn't be replaced. Here is a dandy way to clean them yourself very inexpensively. Wipe the seats with a cloth wrung from a solution made as follows: Place a quart of boiling water in the top of your double boiler, add 3 tablespoons of boiled linseed oil and 1 tablespoon of turpentine. Put boiling water in the bottom of the double boiler to keep the solution hot, but do not place this mixture directly over the flame.

After the cleaning job is done, coat the seats on both sides with clear satin varnish to preserve and protect them from further grime and soil.

You can put old beaten-up *tables* back into service by covering them attractively—to the floor. Cut a circle with a diameter twice the height of the table from any fabric that harmonizes with your room. Use chalk to mark the circle. Working on the floor, hem the circle with fringe and you will have a decorator piece with many uses.

If those table pads slide around on your dining room table, buy a sheet of foam plastic (the ¼-inch thick size is ideal for this), and glue it to the underside of the pads. This will not only stop the pads from sliding around, but also gives your table added protection.

• • •

An expert, Ken Doucette, says: "To separate two drinking *glasses* that have stuck together, fill the inside glass with cold water and set the outer one in warm water. By contraction and expansion, they will separate easily." It really works!

When washing your good *glassware*, use a toothbrush to reach into any hard-to-get-at crevices where dust settles and dulls the brightness. This is also dandy for those crystal chandeliers.

If a *glass vase* or carafe gets cloudy, fill it with vinegar and add a few tea leaves. Shake until the glass is clear.

Did you know that *glue* works much more effectively in warm temperatures? Thus, it isn't a good idea to do your gluing repair jobs in a cold or unheated garage.

A thin film of glue makes a stronger joint than a thick film.

When your paste glue has hardened, soften it with a few drops of vinegar.

Winter is a good time to spray-paint those *golf balls*— especially if you are eagerly awaiting another trip to the golf course. Use egg cartons to hold the golf balls while you spray them with colored paint. When one side dries, turn and spray the other side. Choose any color. Yellow makes for a ball that is easily found in the grass (or sand).

Tighten a loose *hammer handle* by soaking it in linseed oil for several hours or overnight. It will swell to its original fit.

Or, let it stand in a pail of water overnight. The wood will expand and the handle will automatically tighten.

Many people have a worn *iron cord* repaired professionally (even though it costs a bit) because it sounds tricky.

Actually, it isn't difficult to do yourself. At the back of the iron, where the cord disappears into the handle, you will find some screws holding a little plate in place. Remove these screws, and you will discover that the iron cord splits in two inside, with each wire going to a post and held on by a small nut. Remove the two nuts, and the cord comes off. Take the cord to an electrical repair shop and ask the dealer for one just like it. To put in the replacement, reverse the procedure by which you removed it. There's really no trick to it at all!

Do dull *kitchen implements* plague you? Here is a simple way to sharpen them yourself. For a French fry cutter, take a small, tapered, triangular file and file against the edge with careful, short, even strokes. This will work for most utensils with a similar cutting edge. You can even sharpen the metal four-sided grater you use when cutting cabbage for slaw using a small, tapered rattail file. Work from the inside out.

Keep those woven covers on your *lamp cords* from fraying in the following manner: Thin a bit of colorless shellac and apply two coats to the 2 inches of cord nearest the plug.

Lampshade Repair

Parchment lampshades should be conditioned occasionally with a good leather conditioner or castor oil to keep them from becoming brittle and dry.

Those parchment lampshades can also be renovated by painting the insides with a white rubber-base paint. Be sure to apply the paint evenly, as often the brush strokes and unevenness do not show until the light is turned on. To insure a professional job, give the shade two coats instead of one.

Why not dye that faded or waterstreaked *fabric* lampshade? Choose a container large enough to allow you to immerse the entire shade at once. Have your dye mixture good and hot, then dip the shade in and out of the dye until you achieve the desired color. Keep in mind that the lampshade will be lighter in color after it has dried than when it is wet. Also, the color you are using should be considerably darker than the streaks you are trying to cover.

When you are pleased with the color, dip the entire shade in and out of cold water to remove the extra dye. Set aside to dry.

Ever have a *dent* in a lampshade? Try this: Wipe the inside of the shade where the crease is with a slightly damp cloth. Be sure the cloth is wrung out as much as possible, or this will not work. Gently ease the dent right out of the lampshade.

• • •

When magnetic *locks* become faulty and cabinet doors will not stay shut, purchase some 1" × 2" magnets and insert them between the doors and the cabinet frames. You will find they work beautifully.

Lubrication of household appliances—fans, electric mixers, electric can openers, etc.—is best accomplished by using a medicine dropper. Too much oil is as bad as too little, and squirting oil indiscriminately might "gum up the works."

Luggage Care and Repair

When you take those suitcases out of your storage area, there is much that can be done to prepare them for traveling—considerably lengthening their life as well as enhancing their appearance. *Leather suitcases* can be rejuvenated by using one of the new shoe leather dyes now on the market. Use the leather conditioner that comes with the dye to remove all surface dirt and grime. After applying the leather dye, put on a few coats of good paste wax, buffing well until a high gloss is attained.

The manufacturers of *vinyl luggage* suggest that these items be cleaned in the following manner: Use a gentle soap and warm water, rinsing well. Or use a cleaning preparation such as a window cleaning spray. If stubborn stains refuse to disappear, try butylcellusolve, which can be purchased at any paint store. When using the latter product, be sure to use a bath towel, as it will dissolve a cellulose sponge, leaving the gummy residue on anything it touches.

A small drop of baby oil or olive oil on the *locking mechanism* will keep these latches working smoothly.

If you would like to *wax* your vinyl luggage after cleaning, any good silicone-base automobile or furniture polish will preserve the luster. Manufacturers recommend that a combination cleaner–polish not be used.

Should the luggage have an odor of *mildew* or a musty smell, try spraying the inside with deodorant and leave the bag closed for a few days. Thereafter, put a small piece of perfumed soap in each pocket before storing between trips.

• • •

You can add new life to your *measuring tape* by ironing it between two sheets of waxed paper.

To mend a *mirror* that has a scratch on the back, smooth a piece of aluminum foil the size of the scratch over the back of the mirror. Coat with shellac and allow to dry. The mark will disappear.

How can you clean an old, gummy *nail file?* Paint it with cuticle remover, and leave this on for a day. Then, wash it off. All the grime will adhere to the remover. (It's the pennies we save on things like a nail file that add up to the dollars for a new color television set.)

When those smart, big *paper flowers* so popular for decorating today start to get droopy and out of shape, spray them with hair spray until they are nice and moist. Set them in separate jars to dry after you have gently re-shaped and straightened them. They will look crisp, perky, and shapely.

Quickly sharpen that dull *pencil sharpener* by holding a piece of sandpaper against the cutter and turning the handle backward.

Do you have an old *picture frame* which is too far gone to be patched and refinished? Cover it with apricot or peach stones and paint with copper-colored lacquer.

Do you find yourself continually straightening the *pictures* hanging on your walls? Put a stop to the slipping and sliding by winding a strip of adhesive tape around the picture hook. Now, the wire cannot slide—tilting the picture askew.

You can easily remove dents from *ping pong balls* by boiling them in water for a few minutes.

You can mend a *plastic pail* so that it will hold water once again. Cut a piece of plastic from another old pail or plastic item, heat your electric soldering iron, and melt the plastic patch onto the hole in the pail.

Plastic *placemats* with a "linen" or texture finish can often collect stains and ugly discoloration. Scouring will oftentimes wear off the designs and colors. Pre-treat the place mats with Jubilee Kitchen Wax and make them more stain resistant and easier to clean.

Plumbing

What can be more annoying to a busy housewife than a *clogged drain?* When this happens we make a firm resolution to hereafter drop a few drain-cleansing crystals into its gaping mouth each week—as the plumbers and manufacturers recommend. But, our resolution doesn't do much to help a drain which has already become clogged. There are many commercial products on the market which unclog drains effectively, and they all recommend that the housewife follow the instructions on the can or bottle explicitly. But . . . do they ever tell us what will happen if we *don't* follow their instructions to the letter? Never. So—let me tell you.

Plumbers tell us the drain which most often becomes clogged is the one in which the automatic clothes washer empties. A nylon stocking tied to the drain hose will catch an amazing amount of lint—even if your machine has a lint trap. Of course, you can't beat a strainer in the drain. I had neither of these devices, and my utility room drain was plugged . . . but good. (So well, in fact, that as chief bailer it was interesting to note that each cycle the washing machine went through contained 11 pails of water.) When the bottom of the sink could finally be seen, I sprinted for the can of drain cleaner. The directions said: "Use 2 tablespoons—repeating the procedure if necessary, but *never* use more than 4 tablespoons." Well, if 4 tablespoons would do the trick, just think what the whole can would do? Down the hole I sent it. It gurgled, bubbled, boiled, and threw enough gagging smoke into the air to put one in mind of Mount Vesuvius about to you-know-what. This prompted a hasty trip to the wastebasket to retrieve the empty can and re-read the instructions. Since nothing was mentioned about a possible explosion, there was little to do but wait for the required "10 minutes—then flush thoroughly with cold water." Here, again, the housewife "goofed." This sink was really clogged, so why not let the cleansing solution "work" for 20 minutes instead of 10 before flushing?

When the professional plumber came in, he found what he called a "frozen pipe." This means the drain cleaner, which had not been rinsed down in 10 minutes, had turned into a substance best described as "cement." Since it could not be chipped, cracked, or budged in any way, the pipe had to be replaced. Now we know *why* the manufacturer warns against using more than 4 tablespoons—not that it was dangerous . . . just a bit expensive!

And all this just because I didn't have a nylon stocking tied to the hose? Nope. Before the captain of this ship could wag a finger in disdain, the plumber pulled out a handful of feathers. It seems as though somebody thought the utility room sink would be a dandy place to clean his ducks after the last hunting trip.

Without spending a cent, you can easily remove the mineral deposits that may clog a *shower head* in hard-water areas. Unscrew the head, place it in a pan, and cover it with vinegar. Bring the vinegar to a boil and simmer for 15 to 20 minutes. Cool, rinse in cold water, and replace the unclogged shower head!

Here is a dandy trick to use when the kitchen *sink* is clogged and you don't have a plunger. Take a plastic lid from a three-pound coffee can and lay it flat over the drain opening. Then push up and down rapidly with the palm of your hand. The same job will be accomplished that would have been done with a plunger.

Rare is the housewife who has a handyman at her beck and call . . . so the plumbing experts warn us to learn to turn off those water faucets gently. Every time you wrench the handle roughly, you are applying undue wear on the rubber washer, which will cause the pipes to vibrate, resulting in a leaky water faucet!

Did you know you can very easily fix that clogged *faucet* yourself? The faucets in most sinks and lavatories have a special fitting that mixes water and air so that the stream is not so powerful or dense that it splashes. Inside this fitting are two or more circular screens or filters. When these clog with sediment which is almost invisible, as they all do in time, the antisplash feature is done—and the stream often goes haywire.

Unscrew the small fitting at the end of the faucet. This can sometimes be loosened by hand. If not, use pliers. Take out the screens or filters and rinse them individually under a hard stream of water. If necessary, use an old toothbrush to loosen the sediment. Then put the screens and fitting back on for a perfectly working faucet again. Just one word of caution. To be sure of proper operation, notice the order in which the screens came out and put them back in the same sequence.

● ● ●

Postage stamps that have become stuck to one another can be "unstuck" if you will place them in the freezing compartment of your refrigerator for about an hour.

When you have lost a knob on a *pot lid*, put a sharp-pointed screw through the hole in the lid, and fix on a cork to replace the knob. Come up from underneath, and twist the screw into the cork. This will make a fairly good heat-proof knob, extending the life of the pot.

As soon as you notice a chip in white *pottery*, coat the roughened surface with nail polish. Sealed this way, the exposed porous clay can't absorb dust and stains which make the chip conspicuous.

Drill bits and *power saw blades* will cut more smoothly when rubbed with soap occasionally.

You can make your *razor blades* last much longer if you take a jar large enough to hold your razor, fill it with enough mineral oil to cover the head of the razor, and keep your razor in it when not in use. Rinse the razor after each use—before returning to the jar—and be sure your jar has a tight-fitting lid.

Ever find that a *rope*, left idle in cold weather or over the course of a season, had become stiff and hard to use? Try soaking it in hot, soapy water until if has softened and regained some of its original flexibility. Then, after it has dried, apply a light coating of linseed oil. The linseed helps the line to retain its pliability longer.

If you use *rubber gloves* for most household chores, there is no need to discard them because they have a small rip. Those plastic patches sold to repair swimming pools do an excellent job. Turn the glove inside out and place the patch over the rip, to make your gloves like new.

Those of us who use rubber gloves, have no doubt found that long fingernails raise havoc with the gloves and the budget. Next time, don a pair of old cloth gloves, then put the rubber gloves over them. You will be amazed at how long they will last.

Rug and Carpet Care

If your *shag rugs* begin to lose their bounce after several washings, turn them face down on a flat surface and coat them with a liquid starch solution. Use twice the amount of starch needed for the heaviest solution recommended by the manufacturer. Let the rugs dry thoroughly, and watch them retain their original shapes!

It will take a little work, but you *can* fluff up that matted *scatter rug*. Plug in your steam iron and hold it about 6 inches above the matted carpet. Brush as you move along, with a stiff whisk broom or a wire brush. This method will not only fluff your matted rug, but it actually seems to brighten the colors.

If you are in a big hurry, it might help to run your carpet sweeper (moving in one direction only) over the entire rug. When you come to the edge, lift the sweeper up and start again at the opposite side of the rug, instead of pulling it back. Best results can be obtained by moving in the direction opposite to the way the pile lies.

When that *throw rug* in the bathroom begins to slip, don't pitch it. Sew an old bath mat on the underside of it. Not only will this give new body to the throw rug, but you can turn it over and step on it when emerging from the tub.

If the corners of a *fiber rug* have curled, you can flatten them easily with a length of wire which has been inserted into the hem of the rug. The wire can be bent into any direction, straightening the rug whether it is round, oval, or square in shape.

Clear plastic fishing line is excellent for sewing *braided rugs* together when they have split apart. It won't wear out or break, and your rug will last a lot longer.

One housewife tells us that this is the way she fixes a *cigarette burn* in carpeting: Brush the burned spot. Using sandpaper, rub off the remaining charred threads. Spread a small amount of glue evenly across the spot. While the glue sets, lightly scrape the top of the surrounding carpeting with a razor blade (or use any leftover carpet pieces for this purpose). Place the scrapings on the spot, and tap gently. Let this dry several days—and you will have an acceptable repair job.

When that *stair carpeting* begins to ravel along the sides, you can get several years more wear out of it by doing the following: Neatly trim the edges, then apply white household adhesive that dries clear. Repeat this procedure about three times, allowing a day for complete drying between each application. A firm edge will be formed that will last for quite awhile. You might want to slip a piece of shirt cardboard between the carpet and the stairs to insure that the carpet won't stick to the steps.

• • •

A house full of dull *scissors* can be very frustrating. You can sharpen them very quickly by cutting through a sheet of fine sandpaper!

Use extreme care if you try to sharpen your scissors on your electric knife sharpener. Unless they are sharpened at precisely the right angle, they can be badly damaged. Usually a knife sharpener will not effectively sharpen scissors unless it has an extra slot marked especially for scissors.

Rid those wire *scouring balls* of imbedded grease by placing them in the automatic dishwasher.

Ever try mending the torn corners of fitted *sheets?* Next time, use parts cut from an old two-way stretch undergarment. You will be amazed at how well this works.

Here is another idea for those sheets. When your white sheets get that "tired" look, buy some all-purpose dye (the kind that can be used in the automatic washer) and enjoy snoozing on your favorite color. Dye pillowcases to match.

You can easily repair a broken glass *shelf* in your medicine cabinet. Try replacing it, and the rest of the shelves, with unbreakable ⅛" thick hardboard (available at any lumber yard and some hardware stores). If you can, get the kind that is smooth on both sides. Cut each shelf to size from the hardboard, using the corresponding glass shelf as your pattern. Sand the edges and round off the corners. You can spray or brush-paint these shelves, or cover them with adhesive-backed paper if you desire.

Reinforce the bottom of your *shopping bag* with a lid from a shoe box for longer wear and service.

Here is a dandy way to repair holes in plastic items such as *shower curtains*, plastic tablecloths, curtains, etc. Take a piece of excess plastic and cut a "patch" somewhat larger than the hole. Then, put a piece of waxed paper on your ironing board, placing the plastic item and the patch on top of it. Put another piece of waxed paper on top. Heat your iron to "wash and wear," then unplug it. Rotate the iron around on the waxed paper over the patched area, being careful not to touch the plastic material. The waxed paper will protect the plastic and you can still see what you are doing. When the patch is bonded to the fabric, pull off the waxed paper.

Many homemakers find that the holes that the rings go through in the shower curtains tear quite easily, shortening the life of the curtain. When this happens to you, sew a strip of bias binding to match the shower curtain across the entire width, just above the holes. You will find it will never tear, and even adds to the appearance of the shower curtain.

Here is a way to do an effective repair job on those plastic shower curtains, tablecloths, kitchen appliance covers, or plastic storage bags that contain mildewed spots. Brush off the mildew as best as you can, then wash in a solution of 1 gallon of water, ½ cup of chlorine bleach, and a small amount of detergent. Use your automatic washer for the job, turning to the shortest cycle. Tumble dry without heat, and chances are most—if not all—of the mildew will disappear.

Those *smoke detectors* in your home should be checked at least once a month. Light a match, extinguish it, then hold it up to the detector. The smoke will activate the alarm.

We sometimes forget that those all-handy *sponges* can be washed. The secret is to wash them before they become too soiled. For instance, the sponge you use daily in the kitchen can be tucked into the silverware section of your dishwasher. Or, sponges can be freshened by soaking overnight in salt water.

Here is a method for removing mustard stains from your good white *tablecloth*—or even from a vinyl cloth used for picnics. Rub glycerin on the stain, then wash with detergent and warm water. Don't despair when the mustard spot turns red from the glycerin! This will come out in the wash.

When your best white tablecloths begin to show their age in the form of small pinholes, don't darn them. Purchase a remnant of a large flower print, or one with geometric shapes, and use the print for appliqués. Cut out the figures, then with the zigzag on your sewing machine, attach the flowers over the pinholes, adding a few here and there to balance the design.

If the plastic clips that hold your *television trays* have broken, you can fix them by buying spring-type clamps (the kind that are used for holding brooms, mops, and other round-handled objects). Rivet them to the underside of the trays and they will be firm enough for the roughest use.

When your *tennis balls* have lost their bounce, wrap them in foil and pop them into the oven for 20 minutes at 200 degrees. They will be good for at least 15 more games!

To prolong the life of your *tennis racket strings*, coat them with petroleum jelly before storing.

When needles finally punch holes in the end of a

perfect-fitting *thimble*, put two drops of quick-drying glue into the thimble, then the head of a thumb tack (convex side down), and push it in until it is solid. Let this dry for two days, and your thimble will give you many more years' wear.

Your craft *tools*, oiled or greased, won't rust and dry out if you cover them with foil after each use.

Toss several mothballs into that toolbox to absorb moisture and prevent rust.

You can use the very last bit of *toothpaste* in the tube if you hold the tube under hot water, then squeeze.

Don't wait for those *bath towels* to wear out and become frayed at the edges. At the first sign of wear, stitch matching bias tape to the bottoms and tops of the towels. This will lengthen their life by many months.

Stubborn grease stains can easily be removed from dishcloths and *dish towels* if you put water on them, sprinkle with scouring powder or kitchen cleanser, and rub together briefly before washing in hot, sudsy water.

You can revive *tweezers* that have lost their grip with an ordinary emery board. Grasp the board with the tweezers, then move the tweezers back and forth briskly. Alternate the emery board's fine and coarse edges during the process.

No need to purchase a new *umbrella* when ribs pull out at the tips. Simply dab a little colorless nail polish into the empty space and force the ribs back into place. When dry, they will stay in place indefinitely.

Here is a tip for the day when the hose on your *vacuum cleaner* breaks and you cannot replace it before you need to use the cleaner. Take a 3-inch piece of cardboard tube from a waxed paper roll, split it open and wrap it around the hose like a splint. Then use plastic electrical tape to wrap the entire hose section, extending the tape beyond the ends of the cardboard. You will find it works very well.

When your vacuum cleaner bag springs a hole, and you don't have time to purchase a new one right away, turn the bag wrong-side out and apply an iron-on tape patch. A folded towel placed behind the tape will prevent the two sides of the bag from sticking together as you are ironing on the patch.

When your *vaporizer* gets clogged with lime deposits, don't pitch it. Pour about a cup of vinegar into the vaporizer, fill it with water, and watch the lime deposits diminish as the steam is forced through. It will work like new!

Don't throw away that lovely *vase* just because it has developed a crack. It can be lined with foil to prevent leaking.

You can easily repair a broken *venetian blind* tape with adhesive tape on the reverse side. Wipe the tape with a small amount of white shoe polish applied with a sponge, and it will look as good as new.

When the hinges on your *waffle iron* or electric broiler are not functioning properly, apply petroleum jelly. Do the same for hinges on your refrigerator doors, cabinet doors, oven door, and even your car doors!

To remove that burned-on grease from a waffle iron, place a cloth rung lightly out of ammonia (wear rubber gloves for this job) in the waffle iron. Close the cover and leave overnight. Next morning, rub lightly with steel wool, heat the iron and let the odor of the cleaning agents burn off.

If your *windows* are difficult to open, spray the groove with an aerosol furniture wax.

Here is a dandy way to mend a torn *window screen:* Cut out a piece of screen about an inch larger than the hole all around. Strip down the edges until you have an inch or more of loose wires hanging all around. Put this patch over the *outside* of the hole and weave the loose wires into the screen. You will not only have a bug-proof window, but the patch will be fairly inconspicuous if the job is done with care.

How many times have we gone out and bought new roller-type *window shades* because the old ones would not roll up and down properly? Even though you might suspect the springs on the shade are broken, try oiling the ends of each roller on the springs before throwing it away. Take down the blind when you do this. Chances are, you will be surprised to see that the shade has many years of service left in it!

There is no need to replace those soiled window shades, when they can be quickly and easily cleaned by spreading them out on a table—or the floor—and rubbing them with wallpaper cleaner. A sponge dipped in warm suds will also do an effective job. Be sure to overlap your strokes for a fine, even result. If the resulting job still doesn't seem adequate, why not restore them by covering with decorative adhesive-backed paper?

To tighten a window shade, remove it from the window, put the wide-pronged end in an old-fashioned keyhole and turn to the necessary tightness.

Wood screw loose? Unscrew it; whittle a sliver from a kitchen match; stick the sliver in the screw hole, breaking off any excess length; then re-drive the screw, wedging the sliver.

Or, take out the screw, wind a strand of steel wool around the threads, and re-drive.

Here is a dandy way to fix that *zipper* that has come apart. Take a pair of pliers and pull out the two prongs that hold the two pieces of tape together at the bottom. This will allow space to start the zipper up again evenly. It may get a little tedious starting the zipper again, and take a little time—but not half as long as it would take to put in a new zipper. Then, with heavy thread and a needle, overcast several times just above the break in the zipper so that the tab will pull down only as far as the sewing. Be sure your zipper does not pucker, and that both sides are perfectly even before you stitch over the break.

·10·

Save Dollars with Clothing Care

HERE ARE a chapter-full of hints on laundering, stain removal, and caring for your expensive shoes, hats, and stockings.

Cleaning and Laundering

When *spot-cleaning* your dark garments, try applying the cleaning fluid with a piece of old nylon stocking. The stocking will leave no lint.

Here is an easy way to remove those *grease spots* which sometimes appear on dresses made of linen, chambray, and any other fabric which tends to be stubborn about grease. (Many of the new wash and wear fabrics look as though the grease is gone until it dries or is touched up with the iron—when presto, there it is again!) Spread a cloth on your ironing board, lay the stained portion over it and rub all spots gently but firmly with cleaning fluid. Hang the dress out of doors to dry. If one or two spots still remain, a second treatment may be necessary.

Don't let *ballpoint pen stains* ruin your clothes—skirts, blouses, dresses, or even kid gloves. When the stains are fresh, wet a piece of white cloth with rubbing alcohol and rub the stains until they disappear. This will work even on woolen items such as sweaters. However, if the garment has already been laundered, there isn't much that can be done about the stain, as it has already become "set." Rubbing alcohol also works for fresh *lipstick stains*.

If you carry ballpoint pens around in your purse, you know you are always digging to find them. What's worse, they often mark the purse lining. Use an old eyeglass case to hold the pen and protect your purse. If the ballpoint pen happens to mark a pocket or shirt, spray the ink stain with hair spray before laundering. If the stain persists, repeat the procedure.

Prevent stained *shirt pockets* the easy way—by turning the pockets inside out before laundering and brushing the seams with a lint brush to remove all bits of tobacco, etc. Even a half piece of wrapped gum left in a shirt pocket can produce a melted blob that won't come out during the remaining life of the shirt.

Ever have a garment of *leather*—such as gloves or a jacket—become stiff and cracked? There are several ways to restore these items to their original pliable condition. You can rub petroleum jelly on the item, being sure to rub it in well. Set it aside to stand for several hours, then thoroughly wipe it off with a clean dry cloth. (This even works for golf shoes when they get wet and dry stiff.)

Or, you can purchase saddle soap, moisten a sponge and work up a lather with it by running across the leather surface. Work this lather well into the leather item. More than one application may be required, but once the original pliable state has been achieved, follow the directions on the saddle soap container to keep it soft.

Have you ever had a pair of *"washable" leather gloves* that turned out stiff after the first washing? Don't pitch them—here is a dandy way to rejuvenate them.

Soak them in pure white vinegar (no water added) until the gloves are soft and pliable. Squeeze out the vinegar solution, and blow air inside them before leaving them to dry. Just before the gloves are completely dry, put them on, rub and smooth them until they are soft and fit well. If you notice that a slight vinegar odor lingers, dust a little bath or talcum powder onto the inside of the gloves after they are thoroughly dry.

Don't pitch those *white pigskin gloves* when they have turned into an ugly tan after washing, even though the label said "hand washable." Pigskin gloves must be frequently rubbed between the hands while they are drying, or they will become discolored. Each part of the glove must be well rubbed, and they should be put on your hands at least three times during the drying period.

After washing, rinse in water to which you have added a little salad oil or a bit of white vinegar. This will also help keep them soft and pliable.

After having a suede or leather garment *professionally cleaned*, remove the plastic covering as soon as possible and cover the garment with an old sheet or cloth bag so that the skins can breathe. Never store these garments in a sunny room, as the sun can oxidize the skins, causing a change of color.

When a black or brown *leather belt* shows signs of wear, apply a coat of scuff liquid shoe polish. This is especially effective around the eyelets.

If you perspire a lot, you can prolong the life of a leather *watchband* by glazing the inside of it with a coating of colorless nail polish. It will make the band waterproof, too.

Here's an easy way to freshen up *suede* articles such as

purses, shoes, belts, etc. Brush the item with a nylon stocking. You will be surprised at the cleaning job.

If you have a suede jacket and can't afford a cleaning bill as often as it needs it, try this: Take a little suede brush (the kind used for cleaning shoes), and go over the entire jacket. Then, take a washcloth which has been dipped in vinegar and wring it out well. Go over the jacket again with this. You will be surprised at how well it cleans your suede garments.

If you are given a sticky *name tag* at a gathering, do not put it on your suede or leather garment. You could easily ruin it.

If you want to revive those *sequins* on a sweater or dress, why not touch each one with a colorless nail polish dauber? Or, if the sequins are made from aluminum or plastic, they can be cleaned easily with a bit of detergent in warm water.

The cleaning and care of your favorite pieces of *jewelry* can do much to preserve them and keep them lovely at all times. The experts tell us that cameos can be cleaned by soaking them in a pan of household ammonia for a few minutes to loosen the oil, grit, and film. They should then be washed with soap and warm water, rinsed, and dried. Be careful not to drop them, as they are breakable. Never try to dig out the dirt deposits or use a stiff brush on them.

Pearls should be washed with mild, warm soapsuds, using a soft brush. The string should be examined for signs of wear, and if you wear your pearls often, they should be restrung at least once a year. Pearls should be stored in a flat case, and experts tell us *never* to twist them while wearing them.

Never dig around the settings of any stone. Diamonds and other gems can be cleaned by dropping them into a solution made with boiling water, to which has been added a small amount of ammonia. Rinse with warm water, and dry the settings thoroughly.

If your husband thinks dry cleaning removes some of the "body" from his *neckties*, try spraying them with the protective spray meant for upholstery fabrics. You will find that spills can be removed readily, without removing all the stiffness of the fabric.

Those *canvas handbags* are so popular this year, and are always popular with the teen set, but if you wash them they tend to shrink. Use baking soda with a small brush, and rub it on the purse dry. The soil will roll right off.

Open and inspect every garment that comes back from the *dry cleaner* as soon as possible. Then, if a belt or button is missing, it can readily be traced. Many of us have garments cleaned in the spring, then put them in garment bags until fall. If a belt, etc., is missing, it is seldom traceable unless reported right away.

The soft upholstery brush attachment used on your vacuum cleaner is great for getting dust and lint off *wool coats*.

Hanging your coat up in a *restaurant?* Why not slip the hang-up loop over the hook of the hanger? Your coat will never fall off the hanger, and it will be a lot harder for someone to walk away with—mistakenly or otherwise.

There are several ways in which you can save yourself the cost of a *pressing job* when traveling. Put several pairs of slacks or trousers on a pants hanger, then attach several paper clips to the pants' sides to keep them in place, keeping them wrinkle free.

Or, if you find the closet is lacking in pants hangers, here is a dandy way to secure trousers on plain wire coat-hangers. Fold about 6 or 7 inches of a trouser leg over the hanger bar, being sure the inside of the trouser leg touches the bar. Now fold the other leg over in the same fashion with the inside leg material folding over the bar and resting on the material of the other trouser leg. Material resting on material causes enough friction to secure the trousers so that they cannot fall to the floor. This trick is also good when hanging garments in your car.

Did you know that using *sheets* and *pillowcases* for carrying your laundry to the utility room puts great strain on the fabrics, making them wear out much more quickly?

You can easily remove *chewing gum* from washable clothing by first softening with egg white, then laundering.

When you have *lipstick* or blush stains on either washable or unwashable fabrics, try rubbing with a slice of white bread—or softening with petroleum jelly—then sponging with cleaning fluid.

Rust stains can easily be removed from white washables if you first cover the stains with cream of tartar, then gather up the ends of the article so that the powder stays on the spot (as though it were at the bottom of a sack). Dip the whole thing into hot water for about 5 minutes. Ordinary laundering will complete the job.

Before ironing *handkerchiefs*, fold them in half and pull tight. Lay flat on the ironing board and iron up from the fold. This will prevent uneven edges. Continue ironing, and fold as desired.

Grass stains should be sponged with alcohol. If the material is synthetic, dilute the alcohol with two parts water. (Always test colors first in an inconspicuous spot to see if they run.) If the stain remains, try sponging with hydrogen peroxide, testing first.

Use that plastic *foam cooler* to keep sprinkled clothes damp until you are ready to iron them.

A *closet rod* installed in the laundry room will enable you to hang garments right out of the drier, cutting down on the touch-up ironing. It is also great for drying coats on rainy days.

Or, use a long, outdoor *dog chain* in the utility room for those drip-dry clothes. It has a snap at either end and makes a fine clothesline since you can insert the hooks of the hangers so that the garments do not slide and touch each other. (This is especially great for those of us who are too short to hang the drip-dries on a convenient pipe.)

Keep a set of *embroidery hoops* in the laundry room. When removing stains, stretch the fabric on the hoops, holding the material taut for easier removal.

Rubbing alcohol will often remove marks from the rubber portion of *sneakers* and tennis shoes.

Mildew spots on washable clothing should be treated immediately before the mold has a chance to weaken the fabrics. Soak items in a solution of ½ cup liquid chlorine bleach per gallon of hot water (if safe for the fabric). Or, use an oxygen bleach. Rinse well and repeat, if necessary. Follow by a laundering with detergent and bleach.

Summertime usually means harder wear and tear on children's play clothes. If you have a problem with *iron-on patches* coming loose after one washing, try placing a piece of aluminum foil under the garment before ironing the patch. This will concentrate the heat for better sticking power.

Use a steam iron on the wrong side to remove creases from *acetate or rayon* woven fabrics.

Clothing stains caused by *grass* or *ballpoint pens* can be removed by gently spraying the spots with hair spray before washing.

Or, remove the stains by repeatedly sponging with Lestoil, acetone, or amyl acetate.

Here's an easy way to remove the odor of *cigarette smoke* from suits and sweaters. Hang them on a hanger with a sheet of Bounce or Cling-Free suspended from the hanger hook. Cover the garment with plastic and the smoke odor will disappear.

Cosmetic stains on clothing can usually be removed by applying a liquid detergent directly to the stain, if the garment is washable. Repeat the treatment if necessary, then launder.

When *coffee or tea* is spilled on fabrics, wash immediately in cool water. This will get the sugar and most of the fat (cream) out. If some stain remains, apply a little vinegar, keep moist and wash clean, then dry. If the stain persists, try a little hydrogen peroxide mixed with water as a bleach.

When *catsup* is spilled on fabrics, gently blot up whatever you can from the surface of the cloth. If the stain is dry, soften it with a little water, and apply a combination of solvent such as K2-R or Shout. Remove that by spot washing. If a trace of the stain still remains, use a vinegar bleach.

Immediate application of cool water may save a garment that has been *scorched* with a too-hot iron.

If your family members have a problem with *"ring around the collar,"* remember that no matter how clean the neck, the pores exude oils. Before dressing, rub a generous amount of talcum powder over the entire neck. Brush off the excess. This will absorb the oils and the collars will remain clean, resulting in fewer laundry chores or dry-cleaning bills.

Liquid dishwashing detergent is a dandy for applying to rings around the collar and other spots on garments before placing them in the washer. However, you can save on that expensive detergent by putting it in a plastic mustard container. The stream of detergent that comes out of the spout is thinner than that produced by the original bottle, but exactly right for spotting clothes.

Do you spend a lot of time brushing dog hair and carpeting pillings from the bottoms of the legs of *polyester pants?* Just mist these areas and place the pants in the automatic dryer for five minutes. They will come out devoid of hair or pillings.

Vinegar is excellent for removing *glue spots* from furniture and clothing.

To remove *red mud*, wash with cold water—then hot—or try rust removal methods. Chlorine bleach should not be used if the mud contains iron.

If you detect oily stains on clothes when they come out of the dryer, this may be the result of a *fabric softener* that has been added to the dryer. Rub spots with a bar of soap, then re-launder. Don't attempt to remove the spots by washing with chlorine bleach because it could set the stains.

When washing garments made with *drawstrings*, safety pin the string ends through the garment before putting it in the washer. This will prevent the strings from "disappearing" into the garment.

When you leave a *no-iron garment* in the dryer too long, you can remove the wrinkles by placing a slightly damp terrycloth towel in the dryer with the garment. Turn on the machine for about five minutes.

The time usually comes when all *permanent press* clothing needs a good ironing to sharpen the creases in pants, smooth shirt cuffs, de-pucker seams, etc. By this time the garment is usually a little limp. Use spray fabric finish instead of steam to give it added body.

When washing *woolen gloves*, put old-fashioned clothespins in the fingers to help them keep their shape.

When laundering fabrics with a *soil-release finish*, keep the load small so that suds and rinses can readily circulate. Also, use a little more soap or detergent than recommended on the container.

Why is lint-like *residue* sometimes left on the clothes and in the washer tub? The experts tell us the problem is usually not enough detergent. When this happens, the soil is not suspended in the wash water until the rinse cycle, and the result is redeposited soil that looks like very fine lint. Use more detergent. Or, if you use a no-phosphate granular detergent, dissolve the detergent in water before adding it to the clothes.

When laundering clothing that has *Velcro* fasteners, be sure to attach the fasteners together before washing. The fasteners can snag polyester or nylon knits.

Here is a trick for hanging clothes *outdoors*, and keeping the fabrics from fading from the sunshine. Take a sheet which you have just washed, spread it across the top of the clotheslines, pinning it taut all around, and hang your colored things *under* the sheet. They will dry in the shade, and the sheet will get a good bleaching.

Shoes

If you have scuff marks on *light-colored shoes*, an ordinary gum eraser or typewriter eraser does an ideal job of taking them off.

Do you find that when the *innersoles* in shoes become rough they tear your stockings? Just pull the innersoles right out of the shoes and iron on a patch just as you would to mend clothing. Trim it off to the size of the insole and your torn nylon problem will be banished.

Those white streaks that are sometimes left on your shoes and boots from *salt* put on slippery sidewalks, can be easily removed by sponging the streaks with vinegar.

Or, cut a raw potato in half and rub it over the stains. After they have disappeared, polish in the usual manner.

If you love shoes with *rope edging*, Scotch–Guard the rope part when new. If the shoes are canvas, Scotch–Guard that too. Even after being in the rain, the shoes will look great.

Clean those *patent leather* shoes and handbags with a solvent glass cleaner. Spray it on and polish dry with a soft cloth.

When getting your *white shoes* and purses ready for off-season storage, use a "kitchen cleaning wax" in liquid form (such as Jubilee) for the job. It does a great job on either leather or plastic.

Clean those white shoes and place them in a plastic bag to store for the off-season. They will be all ready to pack if you go on a winter vacation, and there is no danger of the white polish coming off on clothes.

Here is an idea for less waste with paste *shoe polish*. To get the polish that clings to the sides of the tin after the center part has been used, hold the tin over low heat. The wax will melt and form a new cake of polish.

When you are out of shoe polish, rub smooth leather shoes with the inside of a banana peel. Wipe clean and polish with a woolen rag.

Spray furniture wax also works very well for an emergency shoe shine.

The next time shoestrings get frayed on the ends so that they are hard to push through the holes, simply dip the tips in colorless nail polish and let dry.

Here is a dandy way to polish your strap *sandals* or thong shoes. Place a piece of plastic or a paper bag over your hand, then slip it into the shoe. This is a neat way to shine even the thinnest of straps.

If those thong sandals are uncomfortable, try attaching strips of adhesive moleskin to the inside of the thongs, and just feel the difference.

Clear, colorless nail polish makes a good protective coating for those stacked *leather shoe heels*.

One lady tells us that her *silver shoes* were in pretty sad shape. She had them re-sprayed, but even that silver began to wear off, although the shoes themselves were hardly worn. She applied glue very sparingly and sprinkled silver glitter all over the shoes. She reports that this method lasted for several evenings of dancing, and it will be a simple matter to redo the job when it becomes necessary.

Here is a way to effectively clean those white *fabric evening shoes*. Go over them lightly with a cloth which has been dipped in dry-cleaning fluid. Then, rub flour into the material, allowing it to remain for several minutes. Brush out with a soft, clean brush.

Thrifty women make an emergency repair on a high heel that has lost its *lift* by attaching a thumbtack to the heel. This little trick will prevent the heel from being damaged until you can get to the shoemaker and have it permanently repaired. (Be sure to scrape the tack with an emery board after inserting it into the heel—or scrape it a few times on the cement—to prevent slipping when walking.)

If your high heels go right through the heels of your plastic *rain boots*, here is a solution. The next time you buy new boots, place a bottle cap or coin in the heels of the boots before wearing them for the first time. This will prevent punctures.

Or, you can fit the heels of the boots with reinforcements made from discarded cotton-lined rubber gloves. Cement the rubber into the heels of the overshoes with the lining side down.

Have trouble cleaning your *suede shoes?* The experts tell us that there are several ways to do the job effectively, allowing those suede shoes to look pretty and give you a lot more mileage. You can carefully use an emery board to remove any shiny spots, then go over them with an old washcloth which has been dipped in vinegar and wrung out.

Or, take an old nylon stocking and rub the shoes vigorously until the spots are gone and the suede finish is restored.

Some housewives use a suede brush to clean off the shoes. Then, they apply cleaning fluid with a semi-stiff brush, working the fluid in well with a fast stroke. After the shoes have been allowed to dry for a few hours, they can be sprayed with a clear, commercial suede restorer. After this has dried, use the suede brush again to revitalize the nap. The cleaning fluid method, however, should be done *only* outdoors. And, if your shoes have seams or appear to be cemented to the soles, be careful not to saturate them with the cleaning fluid. This method will work not only on shoes of any color, but also on your handbags, belts, suede boots, etc. (Always try it on an inconspicuous spot first, just to be on the safe side.)

When black suede shoes have that "worn" look, dilute some vinegar with water, dampen a cloth with this solution, and go over the shoes. When they are dry, brush with a suede brush. This will give them a new lease on life.

If you enjoy knitting or sewing *slippers* for gifts or for members of your family, sew snaps to the inside of the ankles so a pair can be snapped together. There will be no danger of one slipper being misplaced when it is not being worn.

When the *fabric bows* on a pair of shoes become dusty and dirty looking, take an old toothbrush and some warm water mixed with baking soda, and gently rub each bow. Let them stand for a few minutes, then use the brush for rinsing the soda out with plain warm water. Brush a bit more vigorously, and your bows will look like new.

You can extend the life of your *galoshes* if you put a pair of old, comfortable shoes into them, taking both on and off at once. You can carry along an extra pair of shoes to wear at work, when going to a party, etc. This will eliminate all pulling off and on, extending the life of your galoshes for several more seasons.

Hats

Did you know that you can rejuvenate and clean a colored (or black) *felt hat* by rubbing it with a piece of stale rye bread? It really works beautifully!

Or, pack the hat tightly with tissue paper so it will retain its original shape. Then brush it while carefully holding it over a steaming kettle. Not only will your hat look a lot cleaner, but the hat fabric will actually seem to be revived.

You needn't pitch that grimy *Panama hat*—it can be

cleaned. Cover it completely with a paste made of gloss starch. Put it out in the sun to dry, then brush the hat thoroughly for fine results.

When *straw hats* need freshening, try kneaded-type wallpaper cleaner. Use only a small piece, being sure the cleaner is moist so that it doesn't crumble during the process.

You can improve the looks of your *delicate hats* by passing them back and forth through the steam from a teakettle. Shake gently and shape the flowers and leaves. If necessary, press the veils under waxed paper, with your warm iron. Stuff with tissue paper for storing, and they will always look pretty and perky. Some housewives find it handy to store them on blown-up balloons!

Women who have hats covered with the popular *silk flowers*, are often dismayed to find that no matter how carefully they pack and store them during the off-season, the flowers get that beaten-down look.

You can do a fine job of reviving the posies—getting many more years enjoyment out of your chapeau. Take your old hair curling iron, heat it, and curl all the petals to their original fluffiness.

Mending and Repairs

Do your children have *pajamas* with ribbed neck bands that soon stretch out of shape because the tots are not old enough to pull them on and off properly? Make a tiny slit in the neck ribbing, pull a narrow, loose elastic through and sew the ends together. Be sure to allow enough elastic so that the head will go through easily. This little trick will keep those children's pajamas looking like new for the life of the fabric.

When sewing fine material, do the basting with *silk thread*. When you press over it with the steam iron, it will leave no marks on the material where it had been pressed.

Did you know that cotton thread should always be used to mend *leather gloves?* Silk thread will almost always cut the leather.

There are several time-tested ways of solving the *shrunken sweater* problem. Try making a solution of 1 tablespoon of hair shampoo to a quart of warm water. Allow the sweater to remain in the solution for about 20 minutes. Squeeze out the excess moisture, and do not rinse. Place the sweater on a stretcher or press it and lay it flat for drying.

Or, soak the sweater in a solution of warm water and fabric softener. Then lay the sweater out on a sheet, pinning it down to its original measurements.

Some women find success in salvaging a sweater which has shrunk by soaking it in one part of vinegar and two parts of lukewarm water. Roll it in a towel to remove some of the moisture before blocking it to its original size.

If last season's *cardigan* is too tight, stitch nylon blanket binding to the neck and front. Make buttonholes on one side of the binding and sew buttons to the other.

Keep a vegetable brush in your sewing basket for use when *darning sweaters* or other knit garments. You will find the brush holds the material better than a darning egg.

Does *darning stockings* give you eye strain? Paint half your darning egg white and the other half black. You can use the white half for mending dark hose and the black half for light hose.

If your *slip straps* pull loose in the back of your cotton

slips, sew a piece of bias tape across the back of the slip under the straps.

Spray a bit of *hair spray* on your finger when threading a needle and apply it to the end of the thread. The thread will stiffen just enough to ease the job of finding the needle's eye.

A little machine oil rubbed on the *sewing needle* makes it slide through even the double seams when mending blue jeans. No more broken needles. The oil rubs off quickly so you have to reapply often, but it's easier and safer than broken needles.

Here are some ideas for those of you who would like to shorten *hand-knitted skirts* yourself without dipping into the budget to pay a professional seamstress. Two-piece suits are often taken up at the waist. If there is a waistband, you can cut off the elastic enclosure and make a new one (being sure to stitch on both sides with the machine before doing any cutting to prevent raveling). If the knitting is very heavy, you might want to substitute a cloth casing for the elastic instead of making a new knitted one.

If you wish to shorten the skirt from the bottom, be sure to measure the correct hem length, just as you would for a cloth skirt. Using the tight zigzag stitch on your machine, go over the line where the cutting is to be so that the knitting will not "run." After cutting off the excess, go around the edging with the zigzag stitch to make a "binding" and then hem the skirt by hand. Be careful not to hand sew too tightly, or you will have a visible ridge where the hemline is.

Did you know that if you wear a taffeta slip under a knitted skirt or dress, it will keep its shape longer?

When letting down skirts and pants, remove the old *hemline* by using a solution of equal parts of white vinegar and water. Dip a press cloth into this, squeeze out, and place on the right side of the garment. Press with a steam iron.

Do you notice a white line when you lengthen jeans? Purchase permanent blue ink, mix with a little water until you get the proper shade, and apply it to the hemline with a small brush.

When ripping out a hem you will sometimes find a lot of lint collected inside the fold at the bottom. Clean this out quickly and efficiently with a piece of nylon net.

Don't discard a patterned *shirt or blouse* because you don't have a piece of matching material to make a patch. Use the material from under a pocket, and replace that area with another piece of material that won't show.

Don't pitch those blouses that are too short to wear outside a skirt or pair of slacks, yet pull out when worn inside. Take some old stretch bandage and sew it to the bottoms of these blouses. They will fit smoothly under either skirts or slacks.

Many women who have old, soft, comfortable *foundation garments* they hate to throw away should remember that they can be easily mended with elastic thread. Simply thread a needle as you would with yarn, and mend the broken elastic. It will really stay mended!

For an emergency repair when you are traveling, the bar of a small safety pin pinned on the inside of a garment makes a good *emergency "eye"* for a hook.

You can cut down on the cost of purchasing—or making—lined skirts, by using a *"skirt apron."* Some department stores call them "skirt shields." They are worn beneath the skirt to keep the fabric from wrinkling. Most notion counters have them. They are made from waterproof material, which prevents the natural warmth and moisture of the body from wrinkling materials such as silk, velvet, and the new pile fabrics. Worn over your slip, they do wonders for keeping those skirts in shape. (Many mothers make these skirt aprons to be worn under their daughter's formals—the heavy winter fabrics, such as velvet, keep their press much longer.)

When that small piece of metal holding a *wooden button* works its way loose, get a small screw eyelet and insert it in the back of the button. You will then be able to sew the button back on the garment without having to replace all the buttons.

When sewing *buttons* on garments, sew a small button on the under side. It will strengthen the top button and prevent unsightly tears in the material if the button is pulled off.

When those coat or *suit buttons* repeatedly fall off, re-attach with nylon fishing line (double strand). The buttons will be guaranteed to remain in place for the life of the garment.

When leather-like *belt backing* peels off, it can be easily replaced with a strip of iron-on tape. You will find this handy substitute not only works just as well, but is washable, too.

To remove *balls* from acrylic knit clothing, very carefully use your shaving razor.

If your children habitually break the *zippers* on their boots and jackets, apply petroleum jelly with a small eyelash brush to each side of the stiff, opened zipper. No more tugging and pulling will be necessary.

To keep zippers working well, never force them. Close and open with the tab, and always close them before washing or ironing.

Replace a broken zipper pull with a paper clip of appropriate size pushed through the loop at the top of the zipper slide.

Stockings and Pantyhose

Recent surveys reveal that expensive *hose* and *pantyhose* do not necessarily last longer. The secret of good wear is "proper fit."

You can stop a *run* in a stocking in a jiffy by dashing for the nearest can of hair spray! One poof of the spray and your run will be stopped. If it hasn't gone too far, you will be safe for the entire day.

Need to *dry* a pair of nylon pantyhose in a hurry? Hang them on the shower rod and blow dry with your hair dryer.

Here is an idea for those spare nylon stockings that seem to accumulate because there isn't a matching stocking in the bunch. Put them all together in an old pot and make yourself a *"stocking stew."* In with the stockings, place an old article of white nylon such as a worn-out slip, and cover the slip and stockings with water. Bring the mixture to a boil and simmer until the nylons have all reached the same shade. Boiling does not seem to injure the fibers and the white nylon absorbs some of the darker dye. This little trick will do wonders for your stocking budget.

Here is a nifty idea for getting extra wear out of those *pantyhose*, while putting extra change into your purse! When a run appears in one leg, cut that stocking off below the welt. When the same thing happens to another pair, do the same thing. You will have to don two pairs of panties, but you'll have a complete pair of stockings. If the "good" stockings are for the same leg, just turn one inside out. This, of course, is only possible if you buy several pairs in the same shade so that they can be easily interchanged.

Closets

When *storing garments* from season to season, do not store light and dark acetate fabrics next to one another. This can cause yellow streaks in the light-colored fabrics that are almost impossible to remove.

If you are storing winter clothes in *garment bags*, make full use of the extra space on the floor of those bags. It will hold belts, heavy sweaters, purses, caps, mittens, and scarves.

Never allow a *chiffon gown* to hang on a hanger for any length of time. It will stretch. Always pack it away in a drawer or in a box with lots of tissue paper to prevent wrinkling.

Screw cup hooks inside a closet door for hanging beads and *necklaces* to keep them from tangling.

Wrap two ordinary wire *hangers* together with tape to hold heavy garments so the hangers won't bend.
If your wire coat hangers keep tangling on the rods, slip a small, empty thread spool over their "necks."

Keep a *pegboard* on the inside of your closet door to hold belts and purses. If you slip an empty spool over the pegboard hangers, they will be much easier on the handles of your purses.

Keep an empty *wastebasket* on the floor of your closet. Then when you remove a garment, you can place the empty hanger in the basket. No need to push clothes back and forth looking for a hanger. On wash day, take the basket with the hangers to the utility room.

·11·

Second Uses for Almost Everything

ART FOAM HAS many uses. It will stop throw rugs from slipping and sliding around. Placed under your flowerpots and figurines, it will prevent scratches on your tables.

Junior-size *baby food jars* have many "second uses." They make wonderful jelly glasses, or can be great for storing the items on your desk, such as rubber bands, paper clips, or pen points. The men in the family can use them for storing tacks, nails, screws, and so forth in the workshop.

You will always know how many pounds you are putting into your automatic washing machine if you use your *baby scale*. If you have a 9-pound washer, try loading it with just 8 pounds of clothing for a much whiter and brighter wash.

An old *barbecue grill* makes a great spray painting stand. You can rotate the item you are spraying on the grill and the hood can contain the spray.

Don't pitch that baby *bathinette*. It will make a handy sewing table. The pockets are useful for your pins, threads, scissors, and other sewing accessories.

In most homes, the bathroom rugs wear out much faster than the matching *bathroom seat covers*. By sewing the straight sides of two lid covers together, you can make very attractive and serviceable bath mats. Matched or two-toned, they are both pretty and economical.

Or, save those old bathroom seat covers and put one over your dust mop head. Pull up the drawstrings tightly, and you will have a handy gadget for wiping down the walls and ceiling.

When that old *electric blanket* has burned out, don't pitch it. Remove the cords by taking a razor blade and clipping all the threads that hold the wires into the blanket. This may take awhile to do, but eventually you will get all the wires out. Then, cut a hole where the plug is and put a fancy patch-type cover over it. Dacron batting fits perfectly between the two sides of the blanket (most housewives find the 2-pound dacron batting perfect for this job). Your old electric blanket will be turned into the warmest comforter you have ever owned!

Keep the ants away from your picnic table by soaking pieces of discarded *blotting paper* in insect repellent and placing them under the table legs.

Bottles

If you carry your soap flakes and detergents to the laundromat in their original boxes, you probably become annoyed when the boxes spill over in the car. And, most of us put too much detergent in the machine when we carry full boxes. Why not use discarded plastic *baby bottles* as soap containers? One could be used for the detergent used on your heavy-duty clothing, one for the water softening agent, and one for the special soap you use for your finer things. There is no danger of spillage—and the markings on the bottle enable you to use just the right amount every time.

Homemakers today have come up with many ingenious uses for those empty plastic *bleach bottles*. Here are a few: Wash them out thoroughly and let the children use them as bowling pins indoors. Any size rubber ball can be used, and they will have a great rainy-day game.

Or, cut the top off the bleach bottle and punch a hole in either side of the container. Use a wire coathanger as a handle. For this you can remove the lower bar of a regular hanger or simply remove the cardboard tubing bar, and insert the ends of the hanger into the holes you have made in the plastic bottle. Hang one of these plastic baskets on your clothes line to hold the clothespins. Or use them for holding children's puzzle parts, crayons, games, etc. They hang away neatly in the closet when not in use.

Save all those plastic liquid *detergent bottles*. Without rinsing it out, fill one with water and keep it in the glove compartment of your car along with a roll of paper towels. When the children have sticky hands, or if something is spilled in the car, you will be prepared. The bottle will also be helpful when the windshield is in need of cleaning, or for cleanup when a tire has to be changed.

Looking for a neat, dripless container for cooking oil—something that will be convenient to use, as well? Some housewives find that the best ones are *hand lotion bottles* which have a push-up dispenser. Wash the bottle thoroughly after all the hand lotion has been used, and then fill with cooking oil. You will be surprised how easy it is to squirt a few drops into a cake pan. Even when you are greasing muffin tins there will be no spills. The amount of oil you use is carefully controlled by the number of times you push on the dispenser top, cutting waste to a minimum, as well.

Do you dislike tossing out those nice glass *juice bottles?* Why not save them, wash them out thoroughly, and use them for pitchers for pouring milk? They are much easier for children to handle than the gallon cartons, so your children can more easily pour their own milk. These bottles are also dandy for storing cold water and lemonade in the refrigerator.

When that good *bottle of perfume* is empty—not one more drop can you eke out—don't throw it away. It still has another use. Put the empty bottle, uncapped, in your lingerie or sweater drawer. It will dispense enough heavenly aroma to leave a trace on the drawer's contents.

Here is another use for those empty perfume and cologne bottles. If yours has a spray-type top, remove it and place both the top and the bottle on your closet shelf. You will have two sachets that will last for months.

Empty plastic *pill bottles* are excellent for holding bobby pins, especially in your purse. You will no longer have to dig through everything to find them. If the bottle is dropped, the pins won't spill out, nor will the bottle break. These little bottles are also excellent for keeping straight pins in your sewing box.

You can also use the pill bottle, without the lid, to cut holes in the centers of round refrigerator biscuit dough. Fry the little "doughnuts" in deep fat, drain, and sprinkle with sugar. Your family will love them!

One kind of empty bottle that many households have in plenty is the *plastic gallon milk bottle*. Cut the bottom of the bottle off neatly 2 inches above the base, and you have a box, several of which can be used to organize the contents of drawers, trays, cabinets, etc.

How do you clean your house plants? If you lightly spray the leaves with water, using a *plunger-type spray bottle*, you will find that not only are the leaves cleansed but the humidity will improve the health of your house plants. Many homemakers clean their plants in this manner once a week.

• • •

That old, worn rubber *bowl scraper* is ideal for mixing paints and cleaning out paint cans.

Take those *boxes* you no longer have a use for and cover them with leftover gift wrapping paper. This can be either glued or stapled in place. Turn the edges to the inside of the bottom and top of the box, and use the boxes for storing things like your knitting. You will find them great for packing gift candies or cookies, too.

An attractive tote bag can be made from a giant-sized *detergent box*. Cut the top off and cover the box with pretty adhesive-backed paper. Punch two holes on each side and thread on two handles made by braiding together pieces of heavy rug yarn.

Ever try scrubbing the bathtub with a *children's broom*? It's quite a backsaver. Sprinkle your favorite scouring powder in the bathtub, wet the broom, and start scrubbing. If you don't have any children's brooms around, they are very inexpensive at the dime store.

Another mother tells us that her child's *toy carpet sweeper* was lying on the rug, so she used it to pick up crumbs under her dining room table—and it did a very admirable job. Saves getting the big vacuum cleaner out for very small jobs.

That *wallpaper paste brush* can be turned into a dandy whisk broom. You will find it gets into the corners better, lasts longer, and doesn't shed. It also costs less than an ordinary whisk broom.

Those foam *burger keepers* from McDonalds' are great for lunch box takers. They are dandy for foods that would otherwise drip or be crushed.

Those *business reply envelopes* that turn up so often in the junk mail need not be a total loss. Cut off the gummed strips of the flaps of the envelopes. You can use them for labels on storage boxes, notebook paper reinforcers, etc.

Here is a good use for those old *candle* stubs and jelly jars. No matter where you live, bad storms occasionally hit and your electrical power current is apt to be off for awhile. When this happens, candles placed in candleholders can be rather dangerous, especially if there are small children around. Light your candle stubs, allowing a few drops of wax to drip into the bottom of the jelly jars, just enough to secure the base of the candles inside the jars. They will give adequate light and there will be little danger of the candles being overturned.

If the electricity is shut off during evening hours in an emergency, you can get twice as much light from those burning candles by putting them in front of a mirror.

Wood fires will be simple to start if you use your old, burned-down candles for this purpose. Light the candles and set them under the logs. They will burn long enough to get a good fire going for you.

Cans

Are you looking for a cookie cutter or biscuit cutter that can be thrown away after use? Cut the top and bottom from a frozen *juice can* and you will have a cutter that is the perfect size for your biscuits and cookies.

What do you do with those empty cans from *soft drinks?* There are many "second uses" for these items, and here are a few: Remove the top with a can opener, and fill the can three-fourths full of water. Set it in the freezer and you will have large-size ice cubes that fit perfectly in the largest-size vacuum bottles. These cubes not only last longer but keep the drinks colder.

Or, use the cans with the lift tab openers as ash trays on the porch and patio. Cigarettes fit in the top and the ashes are not blown around.

Take one end completely off the soft drink can, and fill it three-fourths full with date-nut bread mix. Bake it in the can and, when it has cooled, remove the other end and push out a perfectly round loaf which will make dainty and pretty slices.

Others use these cans for coin banks, razor blade holders, storing assorted nails, and for making large popsicles for the children. When making popsicles, fill with your favorite juice or beverage and freeze. When they are partially frozen, put the stick in the center and continue to freeze until completely solid.

Don't throw away those plastic lids from empty *coffee and shortening cans*. They are dandy for putting on the *bottom* of the new cans. You will find they protect the paint or paper on your cabinet shelves. This is especially good for the gals who cover coffee tins with adhesive-backed paper, making canister sets out of them. The extra plastic lid on the bottom will prevent rust marks on the cabinet tops.

Here are a few other uses for those plastic lids from coffee cans: Put them under your flowerpots as liners. They also make dandy covers for small bowls and even half a grapefruit. There is even a use for the metal top of the coffee can after it has been cut off with your electric can opener. Cover it with several layers of aluminum foil and use it for setting your hot pans on when cooking—or as a trivet at the table.

Store extra batteries in your old coffee cans. Storing in a covered can seems to prolong their life.

Here are some ideas for those *adhesive bandage cans:*
Use them to store extra buttons and small skeins of yarn that come with expensive sweaters.

Use them for storing drapery hooks.

Keep one in the medicine cabinet to store used razor blades. When the can is filled, simply close it for safe and easy disposal and replace it with another can.

Or use these bandage cans for the children's crayons and chalk. The original cardboard containers are easily torn, but the metal cans keep the crayons and chalk intact even if they are stored in a toy box.

Keep one in your desk to hold postage stamps and return address labels. The hinged lid will keep the stamps and labels from drying out.

If you frequent the laundromat or use coin-operated machines elsewhere, keep the coins for the washers and dryers in an adhesive bandage can. Keep it with your detergent and bleach, so you can tote it along with your laundry.

Keep one in your golf bag for your tees and another one for those short scoring pencils. No more digging for these essentials.

Use metal adhesive tape roll cans to store your tape measure. Wind the tape on the spool and slip the cover over the top. This keeps your tape measure straight, smooth, and neat.

There are many uses for those handy *potato chip cans*. Keep one filled with your picnic silver, another with packets of Kool-Aid, tea bags, and instant broth. The lids also make great coasters to go under your cleanser cans or plants. They can also be used to cover Hershey's chocolate cans and pet foods.

Those potato chip cans are also just the right size to hold ice cream cones. Once the cone box has been opened, they will fit right into the can, which will keep them fresh. These cans are also good for opened boxes of oyster crackers.

Or use those empty potato chip cans for storing packaged foods that have been opened, such as brown sugar, etc.

That empty potato chip can can also be used for storage in the cabinet under your kitchen sink. It is handy for containing small tools such as a screwdriver, little hammer, file, etc.

• • •

That *beer can opener* has many uses in addition to that for which it was intended. It is an excellent tool for getting into detergent boxes, boxes of macaroni or spaghetti, and all those tough cardboard boxes that have perforations and "push here" instructions on them. It is also a dandy tool for removing those pesky weeds that pop up in the cracks of your sidewalk.

That old *card table*, the one with the unsightly or marred top, can take its place as a handsome game table in your family recreation room if you cover the top with an interesting map. This is what you will need to do the job: One large map (larger than the table top); a large bottle of rubber cement, and a brush. Set the map on top of the table, being careful to put it exactly where you will want it to be permanently, but don't trim the edges. Next, brush the rubber cement on the map as well as the table top. Slowly put the map on the table, starting at one side and working toward the other. Proceed with care, as once the two cemented surfaces come in contact with each other they cannot be separated without the risk of tearing the map. When the cement has completely dried, trim the edges of the map and apply a thin layer of clear plastic spray lacquer to the whole works. After this has dried, fasten the raw edges to the underside of the table with tacks, upholstery nails, or a staple gun.

A sturdy *cardboard six-pack carrier* is a valuable addition to a kitchen cupboard. It will hold boxes of wax paper, aluminum foil, plastic sandwich bags, etc., in an upright position. It makes for very easy and neat storage.

Cardboard Tubes

Cardboard tubes make neat containers for the *candles* you plan to store.

Hate to replace *light bulbs* in high hard-to-reach sockets such as hallways, porch, entry, or stairwells? This trick works for many a do-it-yourselfer housewife. Take a cardboard tube (like those on which gift wrappings come) and place it over the end of the burned-out bulb so it is a very close fit. Give it a twist, and the bulb will easily come out of the socket. Put the bulb into the socket in the same manner.

Lovely and inexpensive *napkin holders* can easily be made from the cardboard tubes found inside rolls of paper toweling. Cut 1 ½-inch wide sections, then cover and trim with colored paper and ribbon. Adhesive-backed paper also makes attractive napkin holders out of these tubes.

Now that you have made new napkin rings, what will you do with the old? Attractive pincushions can be made out of them. For the base, cut a round of cardboard slightly larger than the open end of the ring. Cover this cardboard with satin, velvet, silk, or any plain fabric cut into two circles. (Don't forget to allow for the seams.) Cover one side of the circle, turning the seam allowance in, and sew together by hand. (You can also glue them together if you so desire.) Stuff the ring with foam rubber, yarn, sawdust—whatever happens to be at hand. Put your stuffing in a circle of muslin which can be pushed down into the ring, and gather at the top. Then cover the top of the ring with fabric and trim with beads, ornaments, lace, etc.

Those discarded napkin holders will also be fine for holding your electric cords such as those from the waffle iron, frying pan, and coffee pot, in place when not in use. Fold the cord and slip it into the ring for neat and tidy cabinets and drawers. The cords will not become tangled, and if you mark the outside of the holder as to the contents, you won't have to try every cord before finding the one that fits the appliance you are about to use.

If those *slipcovers* on your overstuffed chairs and sofa are forever slipping out of place, try this: Remove the cardboard tubes that come from the dry cleaners on pants hangers. Cut them into sections and push them as far to the back of the furniture as possible, where the back portion meets the seat. You will find the coating put on the pants hanger cardboards holds the slipcovers perfectly in place just as it holds the trousers on the hangers. (Professional slipcover makers create stuffed "snakes" out of matching fabric to be used for this purpose.)

Carpeting

Indoor-outdoor *carpet tiles* make great bulletin boards. Attach them to a wall or the back of a door with spray adhesive.

There are many good uses for those remnants of *rubber-backed carpeting*. For instance, if the children's hi-fi system vibrates or seems a bit loud, put a square of carpeting underneath to absorb the sound. Or, if your portable typewriter moves around a bit, you can easily anchor it with carpeting.

Save any old rugs for use in the *trunk* of your car. Not only will they eliminate noises from any bouncing tools, but they will also be handy for getting skidding wheels out of icy ruts.

Purses can be made from fuzzy *rug samples*. They take only about ten minutes' time—so they are ideal projects for Girl Scouts, Campfire Girls, and the like. Assuming the samples are bound on the edges, hold the sample longways, fold it in half, and sew the two sides together about three-fourths of the way up with clear plastic thread. (Fishing line is also good for this.) The part left open for the top is turned down. You can add a puse clasp which can be purchased at almost any leather company for as little as 15 cents.

Leftover *carpeting* can be a real boon to the hostess who hates trying to remove those water rings left by glasses. If you have an odd piece of carpeting around, cut it into squares and use them as coasters. If you don't have any carpeting, why not ask your carpet dealer for a scrap or two?

If adequate seating capacity is a problem when you are entertaining, why not buy some of those wooden *snack tables* that stack in sets? The tops of them can be covered with leftover carpeting to match the room. This will not only turn them into attractive stools, but will be decorative conversation pieces, as well.

• • •

If you have a garden, save those cardboard *cartons* that come with your soft drink bottles. They are handy little carriers for your pots of seedlings.

Record albums fit perfectly into some cartons that come from liquor stores. The cartons are sturdy and can be made attractive by covering with adhesive-backed paper.

If you happen to have any elegant *casseroles* that are never used—why not put a pretty plant in them?

At least they will be in daily use, and even ferns can be grown in these elegant pieces.

Don't pitch that obsolete mail-order *catalog*. Rip off the cover, put the catalog on a handy shelf in your kitchen, and tear off a few pages at a time for use for vegetable peelings, coffee grounds, and other messy little bits. Very handy—and saves the paper toweling budget.

A clean *catsup or mustard dispenser* is a fine container to hold water to fill steam irons. Keep it handy near your ironing board.

Turn a small copper kettle or unusual jug into a flower or fruit holder for a unique *centerpiece*, or fill a wicker basket with pretty candies or glass balls. Another unusual adornment consists of an underwater garden made from seashells, pebbles, colored marbles, etc. displayed in a large glass bowl—such as that discarded fish bowl the children are no longer using.

Rock lovers and rock collectors can show off their prize finds by making a rock garden centerpiece. Here is how one lady went about making hers: Take an old oval tin tray and paint it with flat black paint. Place your choice rocks on the tray—just a bit off center for added interest. Then, anchor a sprig of artificial pine into the rock pile. Put a small mirror on the tray so it will reflect the tree as well as the rocks, then cover the remainder of the tray with about ¼ inch of sand. Small pebbles placed around the mirror will make the "pool" irregular in shape. You might even find a few little glass figurines to place here and there in your garden, for a most effective and delightful centerpiece.

Keep a box of *chalk* in various colors with your cleaning supplies. This can be used to conceal small spots and scratches on the walls or wallpaper. Select the color that matches and gently rub over the spot or scratch, to hold you over until decorating time.

Ever try carrying a piece of white chalk in your purse when wearing white gloves? Light smudges can be temporarily covered on most fabrics with the chalk, and your gloves will never look soiled. Be sure to wipe or brush the chalk off well if you are wearing a dark dress or suit, or carrying a dark cloth or suede handbag.

Old-fashioned *cheesecloth* is a great bargain (approximately 69 cents for 4 square yards), and you can use it for many things. For instance, it can line the strainer when you are straining soup stock and juice for jellies, hold herbs for cooking, apply furniture wax, and clean the windshield (keep a pad moistened with window-cleaning solution in a plastic bag in the car).

If your holiday turkey sports a few pin feathers, try using a *cigarette lighter* to singe them away. You will find it neat, safe, and quick. Singeing with the lighter won't smudge the skin of your turkey, as most often happens when you use a candle or a wooden match.

Save that *clothes basket liner* of plastic or oilcloth, even after the basket has been discarded. It will make an excellent cover for a round floor fan when the fan is to be stored during the winter months.

Do you have a small drip-type *coffee pot* that you seldom use any more? It will make a dandy container for bacon drippings. The basket strains the fat. Then, whenever you want to use the grease drippings, just heat the pot on the stove and pour from the spout.

If your attic holds an old percolator, use it for jelly-making. Discard its "innards" and use it for melting paraffin. This is safer and easier than other methods because it pours so readily.

A large *comb* makes an excellent miniature "washboard" for scrubbing the fingertips of gloves.

Did you know that a metal curry comb (the kind used for horses) is one of the finest fish scalers ever made?

Here is a use for those *corn plasters* which have been in

your medicine cabinet for ages—and have never been used. Put them on the bottom of your fruit bowls, figurines, vases, even ash trays. These items will never scratch the surfaces of your end tables again.

Do you usually use cardboard for cutting patterns used in decorating and craft work? Try opaque *cottage cheese container tops*. You will find it is easy to trace your design onto the plastic lid and to cut it. This pattern is not only washable but can be used over and over again. It does not wear down from repeated use, as does cardboard.

Do you have pillowcases with hand *crocheted edgings* and hate to part with the edgings when the material in the cases is worn? You needn't toss them out. They can be carefully detached from the pillowcases and restitched to enhance the edges of luncheon mats or even other pillowcases. Some women dye them to match a plain-colored dress, and sew them around the edges of sleeves, necklines, and even hemlines.

Baby's *cup* makes an excellent container for string, twine, or yarn. As you need the item stored therein, just pull it through the spout of this handy dispenser.

Those sheer *curtains* you plan to throw away can make good laundry bags if you cut a small strip off the bottoms for drawstrings. You can then sew the bottoms and sides together, leaving the already hemmed tops to run the drawstrings through. These colorful and practical bags are also dandy for storing the children's toys or for carrying their plastic play items to the beach. Some housewives also use them for storing mittens, hats, and scarves in the children's closets. These bags can be hung from either a hook or a clothes hanger, and such a "mitten bag" can prevent many a search on a busy morning.

There are many uses for those leftover *curtain hooks*,

and here are some: When going swimming at a private or public pool (the kind surrounded by metal fencing), attach these hooks to the handles of your beach bag, purse, transistor radio, etc., and hang them high enough on the fence to prevent them from getting wet.

Or, use them to hang your mop heads, wax applicators, and brushes to dry in the utility room or garage. They also make excellent belt hangers. If you hang them on a wire coathanger with a plastic clothespin placed between each one, one coathanger can be used to hang quite a few belts.

Misplace your keys in the bottom of your purse? Take a brass cafe *curtain ring*, and slip it around the handle of your purse. Whenever you are through using your keys, slip it on the cafe ring, and it will always be near at hand.

Save those old *curtain rods* and use them in your flower garden. The rods can be placed in the ground to serve as props for tying tall flowers, and the curved end provides a place for an identification tag. Or, you might want to write on the rod with indelible pencil or marking pen.

An old *dish drainer* makes an excellent organizer for children's toys, books, games, etc. Use the silverware holder for their crayons, pencils, and scissors.

This item is also handy for storing your cake pans, pie plates, and pot lids in your kitchen cabinets. Or, it can be put to use holding brown paper bags. The dividers make it easy for you to separate the different sizes.

Here is a quick and easy clothespin bag for you: Sew up the bottom of a toddler's outgrown *dress*. Use a clothes hanger to hang it out on the line.

Ever try using a soft plastic *drinking glass* as a substitute for a cookie cutter or a biscuit cutter? You will find that you can squeeze the glass slightly and the dough drops onto the cookie sheet with no mess.

Never throw away those Orlon muffs from a set of *ear muffs*. These can be easily removed from the metal frames and make wonderful buffers for brass, silver or copper. The polishing job can be done a lot faster, as you can use a buffer (muff) in each hand.

Here is another use for those broken ear muffs. Use them for dusting off your records. You will find the fuzz picks up the dust like nothing else!

Or, in cold weather, why not remove the metal strip from an old pair of ear muffs and sew the ear pieces in place on the inside of a chiffon scarf? Your ears will stay warm, yet you won't crush your hairdo as you would if you were to don a hat.

Those plastic *egg cartons* are ideal containers to give you additional ice cubes for parties. Just fill each indentation with water and freeze.

Get longer use out of your *emery boards* and sharpen your scissors at the same time. Cut off the worn edges of emery boards so that the remaining sandpaper can still do a good job on your nails.

The new *fabric softeners* on the market make dandy sachets. Put a few sheets in the linen closet and in your dresser drawers and everything will smell fresh and clean.

An old *fishing reel* can be a great kitchen string holder. Drill holes in the base so it can be screwed inside a cupboard and out of the way.

A *fish scaler* is an excellent tool for cleaning the inside of your Halloween pumpkin and scraping off the stringy pulp.

Those white *foam meat trays* many supermarkets use make most effective camping and picnic dishes. Simply rinse them out immediately after removing the meat, drain, dry, and they are ready to go. You will find these trays seem to keep the food warmer for a longer period of time than ordinary paper plates, and also prevent any juices from soaking through. After use they can be burned in the campfire.

Are you bothered by sparrows or other birds nesting in the eaves of your garage, your air conditioner, etc.? Try hanging from the rafters an old piece of *fur*, about the size of a cat, so it will gently sway with the breeze. Even a raccoon tail will work. The sparrows might give your nesting place the "eye," but they won't come near it!

Make elegant throw pillows out of that old *fur coat*. Use the good pelts for the front of the pillow and velvet for the back.

Some homemakers even save their *kitchen garbage*—vegetable scraps especially—for fertilizer. Dig a small hole in your flower bed and bury it.

Cover the hole immediately, and dig a fresh hole each time you do this. Before you know it, the soil will be built up, paying dividends in bigger and better flowers—at no cost to you.

Those large plastic *garbage bags* have many terrific uses other than lining the garbage pail. Here are a few: Use them for dampened clothes on those days when you just can't seem to get to the ironing right away. Or, cover your hats, purses, and shoes in the closet with them—keeping these items free from dust. They are also dandy for keeping various items separated in the suitcase when packing for a trip. On the way home, when you no longer care whether things are separated or not, use the plastic bags to hold the soiled laundry.

If you plan to buy a new *garden hose* this season, don't throw the old one away. Place strips of the old hose along your garage walls to serve as bumpers for the car doors.

An old piece of garden hose is a fine protector for the blades of ice skates. Before packing them away, cut the hose the length of the blades and slit down one side.

Do you have trouble holding down the plastic cover on a child's swimming pool? Many of these covers tend to slip off with the first gust of wind or when it rains. Take about four pieces of old rubber hose, each about a foot long, and slit one side lengthwise. Clamp the pieces over the pool edge, and they will hold the cover down without tearing or puncturing it.

If you hate to throw away those beautiful *greeting cards*—Christmas, Easter, Birthday, etc.—why not purchase clear adhesive-backed paper and line your dresser drawers with your favorite cards, covered with the paper? You will have a beautiful and meaningful liner.

Hair spray doubles as a fixative for charcoal and pastel drawings.

If you have an old shoulder *handbag* that is no longer in use, cut off the flap, and you will have a handy clothespin holder to carry over your shoulder while you are hanging up the clothes.

A stretch *head band*—either wide or narrow—is dandy worn over a child's full-skirted dress as a belt. If one tie is missing off a dress, remove the other and use the head band as a cummerbund. It will slip on easily, looks neat, and eliminates messy bows and ties. With belts returning to vogue, many of us might resort to this trick for dresses that have no belts.

Save that old, leaky *hot water bottle* and use it as a safe, neat receptacle for oil-treated cleaning cloths and dust rags.

Cut a long horizontal slit in it and hang it in your broom closet.

If you happen to have an old *hub cap* lying around in the garage, it might save you from buying a new garbage can when the bottom rots out of your old one. Put the old hub cap, with the outside facing down, in the bottom of the can. Push down securely for a tight fit.

When storage space is a problem, you can make that *ice bucket* which is usually used only for parties, do extra duty. Use it for a cookie jar. Line the bucket with aluminum foil or a plastic bag and the cookies will be kept as fresh as though they were stored in a real cookie jar.

The round *ice cream cartons* that have small windows in the top are great for holding spools of thread, small toys, etc.

When several children are recuperating at one time from measles, chicken pox, etc., take your adjustable *ironing board* and make a bridge between the twin beds. They can happily run trucks and cars over this wide road. They can use the board for jigsaw puzzles or coloring, and it even makes a dandy make-shift table for serving their meals.

If you detest setting up the ironing board for small items such as pillowcases, kandkerchiefs, napkins, etc., pull out the bread board and cover it with a turkish towel. It will give you a handy flat surface for these little items.

Don't pitch that broken metal ironing board. Attach it to the wall of the garage or work shop, and use the perforations in the board to secure pegboard hooks. Whether you place the board in a vertical or horizontal position, it is dandy for holding your gardening tools as well as tools used for household repairs.

A child's ironing board is ideal to press small sewing projects such as patchwork pieces as you go along. You can remain seated at the sewing machine and the height is just right.

Save those large pickle and fruit *jars* and place them over the small tender plants you want to protect from wind and heavy rain. You can observe the growth through the glass and remove the jars when the plants have a good start.

Do you have more of those small hinged *jewelry boxes* than you can use? Turn them into double picture frames. Just remove the lining, cut photos to fit, and stand them open on the side.

A large-size *juice decanter* is an excellent container for holding your knitting or crochet needles and yarn. Just thread the yarn through the pour spout—and you're all set!

Those *keys* from sardine cans, coffee cans, tinned candy, etc., can be reused as small screwdrivers when you are repairing a radio, clock, a child's toy, or any other item with screws too small to be turned easily with a conventional screwdriver.

Never throw away an odd small steel *knitting needle*. Save it to use as a cake tester. When it comes out clean the cake is done. The needle can be washed, and it is more sanitary than the customary broom straw.

Your outdated bridge or reading *lamps* can also be put to a clever "second use." Remove all electric attachments and paint the lamp. Then, at the next "white elephant sale" look for a small birdcage and attach it to the arm. Fill the cage with artificial flowers or foliage, and you will have a truly different conversation piece.

Don't toss out that old wooden floor lamp base. It can very simply be made into a dandy clothes tree. Hooks can be purchased in various sizes from the hardware store.

Screw them into the pole at various heights for hanging coats, purses, school bags, umbrellas, and clothes for the children at your house.

If your frilly hats become crushed in your closet, why not try this. Take a discarded *lamp shade*, preferably from a small boudoir lamp, and cover it with tissue paper. Make a ball of the crushed tissue paper to go underneath the shade, near the top. Your hats will sit on the lampshades without becoming crushed, and you can make a transparent plastic cover from a cleaner's bag to protect them from dust. Just a glance at each cover will show you which hat you want.

Nail an old *leather belt* in loops around the top of your wooden stepladder and you will have tools such as screwdrivers, pliers, etc., within each reach.

Fill that empty plastic *lemon* (the kind that comes from the store with juice in it), with window cleaner and carry it in the glove compartment of your car. It is so handy anytime the windows and windshield get dirty, especially when you have forgotten to have your automatic window-washer filled.

Toss used lemons in the garbage disposal to keep it fresh smelling.

Those *margarine tubs* can save many a frayed nerve on the tollway. Before starting out on your trip, fill a container with small change so the fees are readily available. You can then place or glue the container on the flat surface above the dashboard of your car, within easy reach of the driver.

If you have an above-the-ground swimming pool with a plastic liner, save all your automobile floor *mats*. Split them in half and place them in the pool under the legs of the ladder. This will help prevent wear and tear on the spot where the ladder is placed. Old dish drainers and sink and bathtub mats are also excellent for this purpose.

Using your *meat baster* to water small plants such as African violets will assure you that the sensitive leaves will not be touched by the water. This is also a dandy implement to use when watering the foliage in a wall planter, to avoid splashing water on the paint or wallpaper.

Treated cardboard *milk cartons* are excellent for watering house plants. They have a handy spout for pouring—and one carton will last several weeks before springing a leak.

Why not carry the charcoal for cookouts and picnics in clean milk cartons? You will find the wax in the carton helps start the fire, and it is always easier to carry along several small cartons instead of a large bag of charcoal.

Or, those milk cartons make fine feeders for the birds. Cut away one side of the carton so pieces of bread and suet can be placed inside. Puncture a small hole through the top of the carton, and place string through the hole and hang the feeder on a tree or post.

Have a framed *mirror* that is not being used? Why not add two handles to the frame and make an attractive serving tray out of it? Many housewives use these mirrored trays on top of their dressers for containing fancy lipstick cases, etc.

Napkin holders have many uses. They make decorative containers to hold a bathroom sponge. Or keep one in the kitchen to be used to store envelopes of dry soups and dry salad dressing mixes.

Here is a dandy use for those old *neckties* that the breadwinner no longer wants. Open them up and sew them together vertically to make a fancy apron. Allow the pointed ends to make the edge at the bottom. Use ties to make the apron strings, too. You will find it a lot of fun to work out interesting combinations of colors and patterns for your "apron." If you so desire, you can line the entire apron with plain cotton to hide the seams.

Do you dread cleaning the grid of a charcoal grill? Here is a slick and easy way to perform this distasteful job. Roll up several *newspapers* and let them set in a pail of water while you are cooking on the grill. As soon as the food has been cooked, place the hot grill between several thicknesses of the wet newspapers. It will steam the burned-on fat and food right off the grill while you are enjoying your dinner. The grill can then be rubbed clean with the same wet newspapers, making it a cinch to wash.

Nylon produce bags make dandy pot scrubbers, and they are easy to make. Lay the bags one on top of the other, fold in half lengthwise, and then in half again. The ends will be inside the package. Fold bias tape over the loose end, and stitch on the machine three or four times to insure holding together. If you make the pads about 4 inches square, you will find them excellent for scouring pans, easy to rinse, and easy on the manicure.

When those *nylon net pan cleaners* get too stained to use in the kitchen, use them to clean the dirt off your garden tools. They will remove it all with little effort.

Ever had leftover *paint* from those paint-by-number pictures? It's really a shame to toss it out, yet if it isn't used within a reasonable amount of time it will harden and become useless. Some women make vases and pencil holders out of ordinary glass jars and glasses with these paints. Tape a picture to the inside of the glass, and copy the scene on the outside with the paints. Or, try an original. Blending the leftover paints can create some interesting harmonies to match your decor.

Textured walls can be easily washed with the aid of two *paint rollers!* This method sure beats using sponges or cloths, which become "chewed to bits" in a very short time, many times bruising your knuckles as well. Mix your favorite wall cleaning solution, dip the paint roller into it, and "paint" it on. Rinse it off with the second roller which has been dipped into a pan of clear water. Wipe dry, stand back, and admire your fresh-looking walls.

A paint roller dipped in detergent suds is also a fast and effective instrument for use when cleaning dirty window screens. Lay each screen over two carpenter's horses—out of doors. Run the sudsy roller over the screen letting the solution drip through the mesh. Rinse with the garden hose.

Save those insulated *paper bags* that encase your ice cream and frozen foods when they come from the supermarket. They are great for carrying cold drinks to a picnic, and for wrapping around fresh-cut flowers when you bring a bouquet to a friend.

Store used *paper napkins* (especially those which are only crushed a bit), and put them in with your cleaning supplies. They will come in handy for cleaning ashtrays, greasy pans, and so on before washing them with the dishes.

A long, thin *percolator brush* is marvelous for cleaning the edges of men's shirts around the buttonholes and the button edges. You can also use it effectively on children's pajamas and clothing.

Slip those *perfumed cards* that advertise perfumes in among your artificial flowers. When rolled up they can be tucked into the vase so that they are invisible.

Or, use those fragrant cards in your stationery box, your purse, or your sewing kit. They can also be placed under the cover of your ironing board. The heat of the iron will bring the perfume into anything that you are ironing.

You can also put them in your blanket boxes and garment bags, especially where mothballs are used, to counteract the odor.

Those old *pillowcases* are perfect dust covers for seldom-worn clothing in your closets. Just poke a little hole in the center of the seamed end to slip the hanger through.

Those pretty *placemats* with foam backing that are no longer suitable for use at the table still have many practical uses. Cut them to size and use for cabinet linings, drawer linings, etc. If some of the foam backing has worn away, you can easily remove the rest by simply peeling it off.

Or, cut them to fit your window sills to use under flowerpots.

Plastic Items

You can protect your bridge chairs and other folding chairs when in storage by slipping *plastic drycleaner bags* over them. They will not only be dust-free, but less likely to become scratched.

During a cold snap, one of the most popular kitchen items can be that box containing the *plastic sandwich bags*. Even if the children are wearing heavy gloves, you may find that slipping a plastic bag over each glove and securing them with rubber bands will make the difference between frozen fingers and hands that are warm as toast. Slipping plastic bags on shoes before they are put into boots will also add extra insulation and protection against wet shoes and socks, and make the boots a lot easier to get on and off.

Those *plastic net bags* that hold onions and potatoes can be great time-savers on laundry day. Have one for each member of the family, and use it to hold their socks. Just tie each bag at the top and place in the washing machine.

Leftover *plastic runners* (the kind used to protect your carpeting from rain and snow) make ideal shelf lining. They can be easily cut to size and are simple to wipe clean. You don't have to worry about replacement, because they last indefinitely.

The square *plastic tabs* that are used to close bread and roll bags are nice little thread holders. Much more convenient to use than winding leftover thread around matchbook covers.

The *plastic top* that holds a six-pack together is great as a yarn palette. Separate your yarns and knot them along the edges of the divider. It will fit easily into your yarn bag, and you can find the yarn you want in a jiffy.

• • •

The *polyester fill* from old pillows can be used to remove nail polish, paint, etc., from your hands, just as you would use a good supply of cotton balls.

What do you do with those little tabs from *pop-top soda cans?* Some housewives make excellent picture hangers out of them. All you do is punch a hole in the tear drop part, then nail it to the back of the picture or any object you wish to hang. You can then hang it up by the finger hole. This idea could save you many a trip to the hardware store.

Save those little pans used for frozen *pot pies.* They are great for melting butter and can be thrown out, saving you washing extra saucepans.

Here is a dandy way to make a rolling cart to carry garbage cans to and from the street, for transporting bags of groceries from the car to the house, or even for toting your laundry basket from the house to the outside lines. Remove the motor from an old, broken *power mower*, bolt a piece of plywood on the top to make a platform, and use the mower handle to push the cart. This can also effectively be used for a mobile garbage can stand.

When the handle falls off that *garden rake*, paint the fork part and attach it to the wall to hold your potholders, big spoons, measuring spoons, potato masher, etc. Or, use it in the closet for hanging belts, ties, and other such items.

What do you do with the *ribbons* from your Christmas and birthday packages? Some families cut them into manageable pieces and string them on the shrubs and bushes in the yard, just as the first robins are beginning to arrive. They then have the pleasure of watching a mother bird build her nest nearby incorporating the pieces of colorful ribbon they have provided—along with the grasses and twigs.

When those *rubber gloves* are no longer waterproof, cut off the fingers and thumbs, then cut each glove flat. Tuck it under your scatter rugs to keep the rugs from sliding, without making a lump under the rug.

A small piece of an old rubber glove placed under the clamp of a meat grinder will keep it from moving on the table.

Or, convert your old rubber gloves into rubber bands. With a pair of scissors cut across the width of each finger, the palm and the wrist. You will end up with several dandy rubber bands of different sizes, with just the thickness you desire.

Salt

Ordinary table salt has more uses than for sprinkling on tails of birds or flavoring the stew. It is a handy-dandy, inexpensive around-the-house helper. For instance:

Pour a hot, strong salt-water solution (cup for cup) regularly down your sink drains, and it will keep your *plumbing* in working order. It also keeps the drain odorless and prevents grease from collecting.

Save on *scouring powder* by using slightly dampened salt on a brush or rough cloth. When used to scour unvarnished bread or cutting boards, it will make them lighter and brighter looking. The same application works wonders on those burned spots on baking dishes.

Scour your *coffee pots* with it. It not only does a good job, but it does not leave an offensive odor or taste as do so many of the commercial cleaners.

Rust stains on white washables? Try a thick paste mixture of salt, cream of tartar, and a little water. Apply the mixture to the stained area, and place in the sun for 20 minutes. Follow by regular washing. Repeat the process for more stubborn stains. This works even on perspiration stains. Use about ½ cup of salt to a quart of water and soak the stained item for an hour, followed by regular washing.

Using salt on your patio or camp-out charcoal *fire* will keep it from flaring up. It's faster and safer than dousing with water and does not rile up the ashes. Sprinkle salt on the top of the coals before you put on your steaks, chops, hamburgers. If you do happen to get a fat flare-up, pour on more salt. The salt is also good for scouring your barbecue grids after you are through cooking.

A teaspoon of table salt and a teaspoon of baking soda mixed into a glass of warm water makes a very effective and soothing gargle. Just plain salt or salt mixed with baking soda also makes a good dentifrice in an emergency. It may not have stripes in it or a mint flavor—but it does the job very well.

• • •

Keep birdseed in an empty *salt box* and you will be able to pour it just where you want it. Use a funnel to fill the salt box.

When the holes of your *salt shaker* become plugged, why not open them with one of those little tie bands that comes attached to the bread wrapper. They work beautifully, because they are really just tiny bits of coated wire. You will also find they won't break off as toothpicks sometimes do.

If you tape a piece of *sandpaper* to the side of your typewriter, it will be handy for easy cleaning of your eraser.

Take that unused *screen door handle*, turn it sideways and attach it to the side of a kitchen cabinet as a hook for your portable mixer.

Many spices and herbs come in *shaker-type containers*. When empty and washed, with the labels removed, these little jars have a number of uses for the creative homemaker. Here are a few: Use them for mixed cinnamon and sugar the children enjoy on toast. Or, use them for containing the salt and soda mixture many people use occasionally for cleaning teeth. They also make dandy toothpick holders. All you need do is shake and invert the glass jar and the toothpicks will tumble out of the little holes. Last, but not least, use them for flour shakers when your recipe calls for a small amount of flour.

When buying *sheets* at the January and August white sales, if you can't find matching pillow cases, buy an extra sheet (which will make four pillowcases) for less money than you would pay for matching sets.

Lining your dresser drawers with discarded *foam rubber sheets* will keep small trinkets, bottles, and jars from shifting into one big cluttery heap.

Here is an idea for a handy laundry bag made from one of your husband's old *shirts*. Sew up the cuffs and tail and hang the shirt on a hanger in the closet. Put the soiled socks in one sleeve, handkerchiefs in the other, and use the body of the shirt for larger garments. When you want to remove the soiled clothes, you have only to unbutton the shirt.

When getting things ready for the son or daughter returning to college, those plastic *shoe and sweater boxes* are a great help. They can be used for holding medical supplies, desk supplies, writing materials, etc.

Empty glass containers from *shoe polishes* can be re-used as handy moisteners for envelopes or stamps. Simply wash well and refill with clear water. You can make an attractive desk accessory for a gift or bazaar item or for your own use by covering the container with a prettily patterned adhesive covering.

You can temporarily freshen the grout on ceramic tile walls by brushing *white shoe polish* into the grout lines around the tile. Use an old toothbrush to apply the polish while wiping off the excess with a damp cloth.

Here is an idea for those discarded *shower curtains*. Sew a heavy object or magnet in each corner and drape the curtain over your automobile when you park outdoors in snowy or icy weather. Not only will you have to spend less time shoveling the snow off the car and scraping the windshield, but you will preserve the finish as well.

Here are some other uses for those old shower curtains. Cut them to size for protecting your countertops when cleaning silver or any sharp object that might damage the surface. Or, make them into capes to protect your clothing when using hair spray, tinting, etc. And, they make dandy beach bags for children to carry damp togs.

The good parts of the shower curtain also make excellent waterproof aprons. They can be cut to any desired shape with a wide hem at one end. Cord or ribbon can be threaded through the hem to tie at the waist.

Use that *skateboard* as a "dolly" to roll your garbage cans out to the curb on pick-up days.

Some thrifty buyers always buy two matching nylon *slips* at one time. Then, when the straps or tops are worn, they can cut off the tops, sew the bottoms together across the cut ends, and have a pair of pillowcases. They wash beautifully, require no ironing, wear like iron, and look very expensive. They also disrupt your hair-do less than ordinary cases.

Here is a dandy use for those old nylon tricot slips and other items of nylon lingerie. They can be made into beautiful *house slippers* that wear much longer than those knitted from wool, and can be thrown into the washing machine, coming out looking like new. This is the way it is done, for a truly professional-looking job:

Cut the slip or nightgown into strips 1 inch wide, either lengthwise or crosswise of the fabric. Wind into balls, and start knitting your slippers on No. 10 needles.

Cast on 24 stitches. Knit plain for 48 rows. On the next two rows, knit together every other stitch. Cast off the remaining 11 stitches. Sew up the toe and front center of your slipper. Sew the back for the heel by holding the two ends together. Alternating colors every other row makes an interesting-looking slipper. Lace a strip of nylon through the top of the slipper and tie a bow in front. This slipper will fit sizes 7 to 9, and the pattern can be cut in half for children's slippers.

If you can't bring yourself to throw away those *soap slivers*, you can utilize them by saving them in a box until there is a sizable amount. Then, place them in a pan, add a small amount of water, and melt them into a firm jelly. This jelly can then be poured into cupcake tins and allowed to harden. When you remove the soap from the tins, you have new bars of soap!

Here is another idea for utilizing those pieces of left-over soap. Save all your odds and ends of toilet soap, and when you have accumulated enough, break them into very small pieces and put them through the food chopper. Use the medium cutter first, and then the fine cutter. To 1 cup of this granulated soap add 1 ½ cups of corn meal and put through the food chopper again until reduced to a coarse meal. Add 1 ounce of olive oil to each 2 ½ cups of the soap and corn meal mixture, blending throughly. Put the mixture in plastic containers. Keep one at the utility room sink, as it is an excellent product for cleansing very soiled hands. It not only keeps the hands soft and smooth, but is perfectly harmless.

Here is a dandy use for the stretched-out tops of children's gym *socks*. Cut the tops off and crochet a zigzag stitch around the edges with colored thread to make attractive wear-ever dishcloths better than those you can buy.

Those *spatulas* that are made specifically for use on teflon utensils do an easy and gorgeous job of removing candle wax from your wooden tables and candlesticks. And they do it in a hurry, without marring the fine finishes.

A piece of *spiral binding* removed from an old calendar can be used to make an eating bar for a pet bird. The ends of the binding will clamp over the bars of the cage, and his treats will stay in place between the spirals.

Does somebody at your house wear contact lenses? Take the tops from two empty *spray cans* and pad the centers with cotton. Mark one "Left" and the other "Right," with a felt marking pen. You now have a safe place to keep those contact lenses when they are not being worn.

Stockings

Save those old, clean, discarded nylon stockings and wear them over your *suede shoes* in bad weather to prevent your galoshes from marking the suede.

You might also try *shining your shoes* with old nylon stockings. They do an excellent job. Or, place the thin part of a clean nylon stocking over your hairbrush before brushing your hair. The brush will stay clean a lot longer. When the stocking is removed, all loose hair, lint, and hair oil will come off with it.

Put a stocking over that soiled *dust mop* before laundering. Tie each end of the stocking, and plop the mop into the washing machine with the rest of your clothes. All the lint will stay in the stocking, and you will be delighted to find your mop does not knot!

Or, partially fill the discarded nylons with *mothballs* and tie the top of each stocking to the pole in each closet or to the racks in your garment bags. Not only is this a very efficient method of mothproofing, but you can readily see when the mothballs have evaporated.

When the firemen or Boy Scouts or other volunteer organizations have their paper scrap drives, use your old nylons to tie the *newspapers* into bundles. Their stretch qualities will make for an easy tying job. And, you will find they are even stronger than twine!

If your *tools* rattle in the trunk of your car, place them in old stockings. This will not only cut down on the noise, but will protect the luggage and other things placed in the trunk from being scratched and scuffed by the tools.

If your family is anticipating a *move* in the near future, start saving those old nylon stockings in a bag specifically designated for this purpose. Why? Because old nylon hose cut in strips and used for cord are much more durable than the light rope and cord bought at the store. They are easy to tie tightly, as they will stretch a bit, and also easy to untie.

There are many ways you can recycle those damaged *pantyhose*. Cut off the leg sections, then cut into strips for use in tying up your tomato and pepper plants. Or, stuff small handmade pillows or animals with them. The waist elastic can be used around large storage boxes to keep them closed, and the panty part makes a great cover for your dust mop or broom when you are dusting ceilings and walls.

• • •

Those plastic triangular *strainers* meant for use in the corner of your kitchen sink are also useful in the bathroom. They fit neatly at the corner of the bathtub and hold your soap, sponge, pumice stone, and even a small can of cleanser firmly in place.

Here is a dandy use for men's worn-out *t-shirts*. Place them upside down in your round wash basket, pull the bottom edge of the shirt around the top of the basket, and you have a perfect basket liner.

How many of us have white lace *tablecloths*, or those of ecru or eggshell lace, tucked away somewhere, either because we are tired of them or our dining room tables aren't as large as they used to be? Try using a tablecloth as a bedspread. Put a pastel-colored sheet underneath— perhaps one the same color as the room, or matching the draperies or carpeting. You will be amazed at how elegant it looks, adding a real decorator's touch.

If you keep several electrical appliances on your counter-top or utility table, you may find you habitually plug in the wrong one. Save time and aggravation by taking a few plastic *tabs* (the kind that seal bread wrappers), label them, and attach them to the various cords near the plugs. You will no longer plug in the knife sharpener to make toast.

If your telephone company no longer picks up old *telephone books*, why not slipcover a few of them (either in fabric or plastic) and use them to raise the seat of a dining room chair for visiting tots?

Your curtains will slip over the rods more easily if you bind the ends of the rods with transparent tape or place a *thimble* over the end of the rod.

Those twist *tie bands* are also excellent for tying together the legs of a turkey or chicken before roasting. No more running for the string and scissors. If the tie bands aren't long enough for a really large bird, several can be twisted together end to end to achieve the proper length.

Here is another idea for those loose electrical cords. Take a discarded *tie rack* and hang it in the kitchen cabinet. It will hold all the loose cords from your coffee pot, waffle iron, electric frying pan, etc. This will keep your drawers free from tangled cords, and leave more room for other things.

So you never got around to buying a hose reel, yet are tired of seeing your hose lying around? Take an old *tire rim* from a car wheel, and put it on a tree or post. You can now reel your hose without it tangling. This is especially useful during the summer months when the hose is in constant use.

Save those discarded *toothbrushes* from your electric toothbrush set and use them—with the vibrating handle— to clean your jewelry and bric-a-brac. They can also be used as a sturdy fingernail cleaner, with soap and water.

Many of us find that none of the attachments on the

vacuum cleaner fit into the aluminum tracks and frames that hold our doors and windows. As a result, the dirt and dust must be removed with paper toweling or a cloth. Why not use that old toothbrush to clean out these narrow places and loosen the dirt?

Buy toothbrushes on sale and use one for cleaning fresh fish. If you don't filet the fish, the toothbrush is the perfect implement to clean around the bones.

Keep a discarded toothbrush in the desk drawer to keep the typewriter keys clean. It is more effective than the commercial variety, and a lot cheaper.

An empty plastic *toothbrush container* (the kind new brushes come in) makes an excellent pastry brush holder in the kitchen. You must try it!

A discarded plastic toothbrush holder is also an excellent container for storing needles. Or, if you make a small hole in the long part of a plastic toothbrush holder and hang it beside your kitchen phone, a pencil can be inserted and will always be handy when needed.

Terrycloth fingertip *towels* make very good napkins. They do not slide off the lap of the diner, are easily laundered, and require no ironing.

Keep a pair of *tweezers* in your kitchen drawer. They are wonderful for lifting and placing tiny decorations on a fancy birthday cake or holiday cake without disturbing the frosting.

Never pitch an *umbrella* because the fabric has a hole in it. Remove all of the material. The umbrella frame makes a fine rack for drying many types of small garments. It can be suspended in a shower stall or set in the bathtub.

Many housewives find an extra plastic *vegetable bin*, attached to the back of the bathroom door, a "must" for those hand washables. It not only catches tossed garments, but is a constant reminder to wash out those daintier things before too many of them accumulate. It also acts as a silent stopper when the door swings open.

If you have some leftover kitchen *wallpaper*, make place mats to match. Use your pinking shears to cut round, oblong, and rectangular sets. You might cover them with see-through adhesive-backed paper for protection.

Don't pitch that old *wax fruit*. Make a dazzling centerpiece out of them. Use colored sequins and ½-inch pins to secure the sequins. Then, starting from the top of each piece of fruit, work in a circular fashion, placing the sequins side by side and securing each with a small pin. The result will be a beautiful new centerpiece to grace your room.

Leftover furniture *webbing* can be very handy in your storage areas. Some homemakers make holders from this material which are most convenient for storing tackhammers, screwdrivers, and even scissors. On the front strip of the webbing holder can be fashioned three or four extra pockets to hold shorter items. Chintz also works well for these holders, and the sides can be bound with bias tape.

Don't throw away that old *window screen*. It, too, can come in handy if you are a gardner. After sowing very fine garden or flower seeds, place the screen wire over the soil. This will break the force of raindrops, check erosion, and keep your seeds from washing away.

Use a *wine rack* as a magazine holder. Set it on the floor, roll magazines to fit, and insert.

Separate the *wires* of a discarded rubber lamp cord and you have heavy-duty laces for your hiking boots. They won't stretch, break, or ravel and will stay tied.

·12·

Penny Savers for Pet Lovers

PET CARE needn't be expensive. Here are some hints for those of you with birds, fish, cats, or dogs.

Birds

You can attract the birds to your yard with an easy-to-build *bird bath*. Scoop out a saucer-shaped hollow in the ground, about 3 inches deep in the center, and line it with concrete made by adding water to a prepared mix. Trowel in the concrete to form a shell an inch thick. Keep the bird bath swept out and filled with clean water, and build it away from shrubs in which cats might lurk.

Or, take a colorful plastic garbage pail, turn its lid upside down on top of it, and fill it with water to make a nice bird bath.

Clean green algae and scum from the bird bath using a paper towel and a little sand, a little water, and elbow grease. (Don't try it on the inside of your fish tank, though. The sand will scratch the glass or plexiglass.)

During the cold months, bird baths should be emptied, as the birds instinctively bathe, even in the coldest of weather. They could fly away wet and freeze! Birds will derive enough drinking water from the snow.

Unused mail boxes make ideal *bird houses*. Open the door for a front porch, then insert a wooden front with the appropriate-size hole for the birds to go in. With a new coat of paint, your mail box can make a pretty bird house to attach to a tree in the back yard.

Do you like to *feed* the birds? Render suet, let it cool and set, then mix birdseed with it. Chopped peanuts may also be used. Pour into a container—possibly one of the aluminum pie tins that frozen pot pies are purchased in—and set it in the refrigerator to harden. Tie with a cord or thin wire and hang it in a tree. Even in the wintertime, the birds will sit and bang happily on the frozen suet cake.

In the springtime, put *lint* from your clothes dryer into your bird feeder. The birds seem to know it's perfect for lining their nests.

Wash and dry your melon *seeds* and save them to feed to the wild birds. Birds especially like squash and pumpkin seeds.

Your children will delight in stringing doughnut-shaped *cereals* on a string and hanging them on the trees for their hungry little feathered friends.

You can make a cute and inexpensive bird feeder by using a large *pine cone*, stem side down. Fill the openings with peanut butter. Use a bright-colored ribbon to tie it to a tree branch outside your window.

Pine cones covered with hardened bacon grease or other fat, then rolled in birdseed or bread crumbs and hung from tree branches or tucked into bushes, will also keep birds happy and well-fed during the winter. Suspending the cones from branches means a heavy snowfall cannot cover and hide them, as would happen if the cones were placed on the ground.

Here is another idea for feeding those hungry birds. Warm bacon grease in a pan. Add peanut butter and as much wild birdseed as it takes to firm the mixture. Place in fluted paper muffin cups, and insert between narrow branches on the trees. These snacks can be ideally positioned in fir or pine trees and the birds will love them!

Dogs

Does your large dog often knock his *water dish* over? If so, place an old angel food cake pan in the yard for him, drive a stake through the funnel part of the pan to secure it, and fill the pan with water. You will no longer have to worry about Fido's being thirsty on a hot day.

Use *baby shampoo* when you bathe your dog. If the shampoo should accidentally get into his eyes, it won't burn.

Cut off the bottom end of a gallon-sized milk carton or plastic bottle to make an emergency *feeding bowl* for your dog.

If your puppy happens to be a sloppy eater, you won't find it necessary to mop the floor after each feeding if you put his dishes in a large *dishpan*. It will catch all the drips, and will also prevent the children from stumbling over the dog's dishes.

If your puppy seems to dislike riding in a car, why not use that old baby *car bed* for him? You will find he can see out the window from it, and if you put his favorite blanket in with him, he will be happy to ride along with you.

Does that new puppy like to *chew* on your wood cabinets, table and chair legs, etc.? Just a little oil of cloves (available in pharmacies) can be dabbed on the wood with a piece of cotton. The odor will probably keep him away, but if he does lick it, you can be sure the bitter taste will curb his chewing.

When *pet hairs* won't vacuum off your carpeting, try running a damp sponge mop over them. The fur will ball up, making removal easy.

Have you ever seen people buying those huge bags of *dog food* and wondered how they store them? Save bread wrappers and wire twisties and repack the dog food when you get home. These individual bags can be stored in the garage or basement, and brought into the kitchen one at a time.

If your dog fights with a *skunk*, wash him in water mixed with equal parts of vinegar. (This also works for people.) A bath of diluted tomato juice is also said to work well.

Cat or dog accidents on the *carpet* demand attention before the soiled area dries, otherwise the stain may well be there to stay. Blot the spot first with a clean turkish towel to remove as much moisture as possible. Then mix equal parts of white vinegar and water, adding enough mild detergent to form suds. Gently work the foam in with a sponge. Then blot with towels.

Cats

You can make delightful treats for your pet cat out of an *old glove*. Fill the fingers with catnip, then cut them off and tie the open ends securely closed. Attach a bell.

Does your cat like to scratch on the furniture? The experts tell us the destructive cat can be curbed by getting him a *scratching post*. You might try making your own. Nail a piece of carpet scrap to a 2 ½-foot long length of 4 × 4 inch lumber. Nail the carpet down on all four sides of the post. Screw the post onto a plywood base and rub catnip into the carpet pile. Some cats prefer to have the post lying down like a fallen log. It's worth a try if it will stop your cat from ruining upholstered chairs and furniture.

Here is an easy way to save your *upholstered furniture* from a cat's claws. If your cat loves to knead the back of your favorite chair, place a strip of cellophane tape on the back of the chair, using the type of tape that is sticky on both sides. His paws will stick to the tape just long enough to take the fun out of clawing. This method will hurt neither the cat nor the chair.

When a tiny kitten shows no desire to eat or drink, get an *ear syringe* and fill it with warm milk. This is easily inserted into the kitten's mouth without danger of breakage. And, the long rubber nozzle on the ear syringe will not hurt his mouth.

Fish

Owners of tropical fish tell us that plain *nylon netting* is the perfect answer for cleaning the inside of the tank. It works wonders for water lines and algae that form on the inside of the tank. (Soap or detergent should *never* be used as a cleansing agent for fish tanks.)

One can also effectively use plain *table salt* (not iodized) for cleaning out that fish tank. Rinse well to make sure no salt remains in the tank.

If your children are raising *guppies*, why not use empty

baby food jars for keeping the baby guppies away from their parents so that they do not get eaten up? The babies can be kept in these jars until they are big enough to go back into the tank.

When going on a *trip*, you can be sure your tropical fish will be taken care of properly if you measure the exact quantity of fish food for each feeding into empty plastic pill containers and place them on top of the aquarium. This way anyone can feed the fish correctly.

·13·

Redecorating Inexpensively

NO NEED to spend a lot of money redoing your home. Here are tips on painting, furnishings, and wall coverings that will help you do a truly professional job.

Painting

Use an *eggbeater* for stirring paint. You can whirl it clean again in paint thinner or soapy water for use on the next color.

Before tossing out that paint bucket, take a *rubber spatula* and scrape the inside of the bucket thoroughly. You will be surprised to see how much paint was left in the bucket, which would have been thrown away had this not been done. This little trick is especially helpful when one is running a little short of paint.

When doing a bit of inside painting, why not slip a pair of *old socks* over your shoes? Not only will the socks protect your shoes, but when a bit of paint is splattered on the floor you can easily wipe it off with your stocking-covered foot.

Another handy idea for wiping up spills is to attach several large *cup hooks* to the top of the ladder. You can then hang extra cloths within easy reach. Dip one of the cloths in turpentine, and enclose it in a plastic bag hung from one of these hooks.

Use a wire *coathanger* to hang your paint can on the rung of a ladder. Open the hanger, slip the end through the handle of the paint can, and rewind the hanger. You can then easily move the hanger hook up or down the ladder rungs, and it will stay exactly where you put it.

Here is a dandy way to take the strong *odor* away from paint. Add one ounce of Vanilla extract to a one-half gallon can of paint and mix well. This will have no effect on the paint, we are told.

If you have difficulty matching the flat paint you put on your walls with the gloss paint you use on the woodwork and window sills, cover everything with flat paint. Wait 48 hours for it to dry throughly, then put three coats of liquid hard-gloss, self-polishing *floor wax* on the sills and woodwork. Wait at least one hour between coats to be sure they are dry and hard. It will gleam as though it had been painted with an oil or enamel paint, and will be so well protected that it will hold up beautifully and can be easily cleaned with a damp cloth.

When *paint spatters* have been allowed to harden on the floor, moisten the spatters with nail polish remover, allow to soak for a few minutes, then rub off with a cloth and wash with warm suds. The paint will usually disappear, no matter how long it has been there.

When painting *baseboards*, insert the lip of a clean

dustpan as close to the bottom of the baseboard as possible. This protects carpets or floor from paint drips.

Attach a *paper towel holder* to the underside of the top of your work ladder. Paper towels can be very helpful when you are cleaning or painting walls, high cabinets, or wood-work, or washing windows.

Before replacing the lid of a *paint can*, remove excess paint from the rim with a cotton swab so the top won't stick.

Experts tell us that white paint is most durable, while dark blue and dark green are the most likely to fade.

When painting a *chair*, place a jar lid under each leg to catch the drips.

An easy way to get paint and varnish off *chrome* hinges and door pulls is to simmer them for a few minutes in baking soda and water. All the old paint and varnish will wipe right off and they will look like new.

An *onion* placed in a newly painted room will soak up the paint odor.

To *strain* old paint, stretch a piece of nylon stocking over a clean can. Secure with rubber bands, and pour the paint through the nylon.

If you are planning to cover a dark color with a lighter color, be sure to buy enough paint for *two coats*.

Hand cream or corn oil, applied sparingly to your *hands* before painting, makes it easier to remove paint stains from them when you finish the job.

Here is a dandy way to lengthen a *paint roller handle* without having to buy a new one. When you want to paint the hall ceiling and stairway walls, attach a steel rod from your vacuum cleaner to the roller handle. This can be easily done by placing a strip of electrical tape around the handle near the end (one thickness will do), then applying one thickness lengthwise. Push on the steel rod and apply one strip of double thickness at the end to prevent it from pushing up farther. Wrap more electrical tape on both the steel rod and the roller handle, covering both well. Press firmly at the upper end until the rod is secure. You can always add the other rod if more length is necessary.

When painting *window screens*, tack a small piece of carpet to a block of wood and dip it into the paint. This method is not only much faster than using a brush, but it uses less paint.

Did you know that if you thin your *exterior paint* with linseed oil you will improve its quality, while adding mileage to it? Turpentine evaporates, whereas linseed oil is a good wood preservative.

You can control the drying speed of exterior paint by adding a commercial drying compound to it. Use more on cool days and less on warm, dry days.

When you must paint a *cyclone or wire fence*, try using a car washing mitten to do the job. Dip the top half of the mitten into the silver paint. Squeeze out the excess and rub the mitten around the wires and posts. You will waste hardly a drop with this method, and the paint job will be completed quickly and easily.

Whitewash will adhere better to walls and fences, making the job last a lot longer, if salt is added to the solution prior to application.

We are also told it is more economical to paint the *outside trim* or walls of your house once every two years than to give it two coats at any one time. Why? Because the job will last a lot longer. This gives the paint a chance to "season."

If you just *know* you are going to use what's left in that can of paint again someday, pour some *melted paraffin* on top of it. It will not gather that thick skin that usually results when paint has been left standing awhile, and you can remove the paraffin just the way you would from the top of a jelly glass.

Paint Brushes

Here are some ideas on keeping your paint brushes in working order—and restoring old ones. A professional painter tells us: "First, examine the bristles of your old brushes. If the tips are curled, this indicates that the brushes were allowed to rest on the bristles for a long time. In this case, take the brushes outdoors, remove the lid from the garbage can, deposit the brushes, replace the lid, and go out and buy new brushes.

"However, if this is not the case with your brushes, they can be restored by soaking in a *brush cleaner*. The powdered brush cleaners are just as good as the liquids, and cost far less. Mix them with water according to the label.

"When soaking the brushes, they must be suspended in a glass or metal container so that the bristles do not touch the bottom. You can buy brush-holders, but you can also make your own by drilling a small hole in the brush handle just above the metal ferrule. Place a nail through the hole to support the brush on the rim of the container.

"Allow the brushes to soak a few days, depending on how badly the paint has caked. Several times during this period, work the bristles through your fingers to separate them so that the liquid can penetrate. After the bristles have softened, use a putty knife to press and scrape the paint away. Using a comb will further break up the paint and straighten out your bristles. Work the comb all the way up to the heel of the brush. If stubborn paint still remains, return to the brush cleaner for more soaking.

"Once the brush is clean, rinse it in fresh water. Twirl it against an old washboard to remove excess water and once again use the comb to straighten out the bristles. Wrap the brush in heavy brown paper to keep the bristles straight, and lay it flat for storing."

Here is another trick for refurbishing a paint brush that someone forgot to clean out after use. Soak the neglected brush in *hot vinegar* for about 20 minutes. Chances are, it will turn out good as new.

Nylon-bristled paint brushes fall apart in alcohol and should never be used to apply shellac, nor should they be cleaned with denatured alcohol.

Buy a brush with *artificial bristles* for use with latex paints. The water in the paint will ruin natural bristles.

When using paint thinner to clean brushes, use a *coffee can*. After cleaning the brushes, cover the can and let stand a few days. The paint will settle to the bottom and you can pour the clean thinner back into the can and reuse.

Do you find *cleaning* paint brushes at the end of the day a time-consuming job? The prospect of cleaning them in turpentine or thinner, then washing them in suds and wrapping them airtight, does seem a bit much, especially if you will be using them again soon. Just shake out all the paint from the brushes, wrap them in foil or plastic bags and stick them in the freezer. They don't freeze. In fact, they will be useable the next day or for several days thereafter.

If your wall-painting project will take several days, suspend your paint brushes in a jar containing equal parts of linseed oil and turpentine. The bristles will remain soft and pliable.

Home Furnishings

Are you redecorating without the aid of an interior decorator and feel unsure about your choice in colors? If so, start by buying a *picture* that appeals to you. It doesn't have to be an expensive painting, but a fine print of a good painting is preferable to a poor oil. Pull your color scheme from the picture. Choose the color in the picture you like best for the walls, your second choice for carpeting, and use the other colors for furnishings.

Spray paint an old wire dish rack with gold or silver paint and you will come up with a fancy *record rack* for your teenager's room.

Ever try using a *piano* as a room divider? Even though most upright pianos have exposed backs, the creative homemaker can cover them in a variety of unique ways. Here are a few ideas: Obtain grille cloth from any radio supply house, and tack it onto the board frame—or directly to the back of the piano. This is the same type of cloth that covers the speakers on your television set, stereo, etc., and it can be purchased in quite a variety of lovely fabrics.

Or, cover the back of the piano with window screening which has been painted. The screen can then be used for hanging pictures or for creating a wall arrangement. Be sure to use porous screening so that the tone of the piano will remain true.

Another idea is to place a panel made of lattice work, finished and painted to match the decor of the room, against the open back of the piano. Woven-cane frames or any loosely woven cloth can also be stretched taut and used for this purpose.

Many a crafty homemaker has made *headboards* for her hollywood beds. Here are a few inexpensive and simple ways to do this, adding an interesting note to the decor of any room:

Purchase a plywood door (the least expensive one you can find), and cut it to fit across the width of the bed. Cut a piece of foam mattress topping the proper size, and fasten it to the door. Cover this with fabric to match the room's decor (fake fur makes a delightful headboard). Now fasten it to the wall behind the bed. You can cover buttons of the same material and fasten them to the headboard, giving it a tufted, professional look. Cleaning is easy with your vacuum upholstery nozzle.

Or, paper the area behind the bed, putting a border all around it to denote the shape of a headboard. You might also fasten four decorative wooden spindles to the wall— spaced at equal distances. Paint these spindles to match the wallpaper, or varnish them for a "wooden" effect if you so desire. You can then use silk braid with a tassel edge to drape lightly from spindle to spindle for an unusual headboard effect.

Still another idea for this project: Take a round gold cafe rod and hang it above the bed just as you would at a window. Using decorative rings, hang "shorty" curtains to match the bedspread as a backdrop for the bed.

You can easily make a headboard for a twin-size hollywood bed out of a folding card table. You will find a card table is just about the width of a single bed, and you can easily fashion a boxed, fitted slipcover to go down over the exposed part of the table so that it not only looks like a headboard, but can match the decor of the room. This also doubles as a storage area for the table.

An attractive chairside *planter* can be made inexpensively by gluing together the bottoms of two 12-inch clay pots and running a dowel through both drainage holes. The top of one pot will sit solidly on the floor and the other will hold the plant.

There are several inexpensive but effective ways to remove old *veneer* from furniture. Here are some of them: Dampen an old bedspread and lay it over the veneer to be removed. Leave it there for several hours, being sure the cloth is adequately wet during this time. Carefully pry the tight edges with a putty knife and you will find that the loosened veneer will easily lift off. Be sure to lift off the glue left on the furniture itself while it is still soft. Some of the glue spots may require sanding.

However, if you are working on a tight, heavily varnished piece of furniture, perhaps you had better start with a commercial paint and varnish remover. Read the directions carefully, as some require water and a lot of "elbow grease" and others merely have to be applied, left to soak a certain length of time, then cleaned off. Either method will make a dirty, mucky mess, so be sure to tackle this job where the cleanup will be easy.

There are several ways to renovate a peeling metal *lampshade*. Burlap comes in so many pretty colors these days, why not take a piece and cover the lampshade with it? You might also want to cut designs from felt scraps to glue on top of the burlap, making the lampshade unique.

Or, remove all loose paint from the shade as well as the grease and dust, then apply a thin coat of white all-purpose glue. While the glue is still wet, sprinkle finely crushed colored glass all over it. Let it stand overnight until thoroughly dry. Crushed glass can be purchased at art stores and hobby shops.

Imagination plus an inexpensive flush-panelled *door* can add up to some attractive new furnishings for your home. For example, put your solid-core door on sawhorses and turn it into a marvelous desk, sewing table, or even a bright new coffee table. Or, using the door as your base, add legs, a mattress, and throw pillows for a sleek modern couch. You might even try a grouping of three hinged doors to make a unique room divider!

You can also turn a door into a picnic table or a unique table for your dinette. However, lumber dealers pass on this word of caution: "Many inexpensive doors have a solid frame only around the outside edges. The rest is made from thin sheets of veneer. Thus, legs cannot be attached except on the outside framing. If you cut such a door down to make a small table or stool, you may find there is no 'in between' where you can attach the legs. Solid doors are more expensive, but necessary if you plan to cut them into pieces needing a solid interior other than at the outside edges."

Wall Hangings and Wall Coverings

Quaint, old-fashioned *silhouettes*, framed on cotton calico or gingham, make delightful wall decorations. They are simple to make. Here's how: Use small dime-store frames, stretching the fabric of your choice over the cardboard backing, and tacking or gluing it in place behind the frame. For the silhouettes, use carbon paper to trace figures or profiles from children's storybooks, magazines, or family photographs. Using the tracing for a guide, cut out the silhouette from black construction paper and glue it in place on the fabric backing.

To complement black silhouettes, use a piece of bright-colored cotton calico, such as red and yellow, in a frame which has been painted black.

Lovely inexpensive decorative pictures can also be made by framing *hand-embroidered fabrics*. It is most important to know that the way the piece is blocked before it is framed makes a big difference in how the finished product is going to look. Embroidered fabrics should be pressed from the wrong side over a thick pad or towel. Use a pressing cloth between the iron and embroidery done on silk or synthetics, and first test the effect of dampening your fabric before you start to block.

If dampening the fabric has no ill effects, you can dampen and stretch the fabric on the cloth-covered board. (Or use your steam iron for this step.) Fasten your needlework to the board with aluminum tacks in order to prevent rust spots.

Here is another idea for an inexpensive do-it-yourself wall hanging. *Painting on velvet* fabric is the latest thing these days, and this is how such pictures can easily be mounted and framed. Cut a piece of heavy cardboard or plywood to fit into the frame. Smooth and stretch the material across the top of this board. Turn the extra material to the back for about ½ inch and fasten with a good, quick-drying glue. Milky white, all-purpose glue works very well for this project. Do the top and bottom first, then smooth to the sides and fasten. Insert in the frame, with the picture against the glass, and fasten with a few small headless tacks. Glue a sheet of heavy paper over the back and onto the edges of the frame to keep out the dust.

Now that *picture walls* are so popular, many of us have been trying our hand at picture framing and grouping. An ideal material to use for the background mats is desk blotters. They can be found in any office supply store and most dime stores. They come in assorted colors and are quite inexpensive, allowing you to make several small pictures or a very large one for practically pennies. What's more, they are sturdy and easy to cut!

When *rearranging pictures*, you can easily fill in those nail holes in the wall by mixing cornstarch and Elmer's glue together. This works beautifully on white walls. If your walls are an off-white, add a little instant coffee to the mixture until it blends in with the wall coloring. For colored walls, borrow a bit of the children's art paint to achieve the matching hue.

Making *picture groupings* on a wall can pose a problem, but not if you cut pieces of brown paper the size of the pictures to be hung. Tape the brown paper to the wall, and rearrange until you achieve the desired effect.

Here is an easy idea for keeping those pictures *straight*. Wrap masking tape (sticky side out) around the middle of a round wooden toothpick and place one or more rolls (depending on the size of the picture) near the bottom of the back of the frame. There will be no damage to the wall or the frame, and the picture will always hang straight.

Looking for a delightfully different wall covering? How about using 12-inch *carpet tiles*? Low-pile outdoor carpeting and the thicker piles (even shag) look elegant, and you will find this a lot cheaper than re-doing a cracked wall.

Here is an idea for making cute wall decorations for a *child's room*. Paint a picture frame red and cover the picture mat with black and white checked gingham. You can then glue tiny black paper silhouettes of animals on the gingham squares, forming your own design. Pairs or groups of these pictures make very attractive wall hangings.

Storage can become a problem when the little ones in your household begin to have a large accumulation of *stuffed toys*. Why not sew a plastic curtain ring or a shower curtain ring to each animal so that they can be hung in an easy-to-reach area in the bedroom? A square of pegboard fastened to the wall, into which the necessary number of hooks can be placed, is all that is necessary to get the accumulation of toys off the floor.

Here is another easy and inexpensive idea for displaying a child's stuffed animal collection. Buy ribbon about 2 inches wide and secure a piece around each animal. Leave the piece long enough to form a streamer, and fasten the end of the streamer to the wall, making a design with the animals. They will look like unusual, three-dimensional pictures. Colored string can also be used to attach each animal to the ceiling with thumbtacks. The large, awkward animals may require two or more strings to balance their weight.

Still other homemakers have saved pretty gift boxes such as the kind dusting powder comes in. Punch the same number of holes in the top and the bottom, then choose heavy wool yarn in a desired color for tying the top to the bottom. Leave a large enough space between the top and the bottom to make a "cage" for holding the animal (the yarn represents the bars on the cage). Slide the animal in and use either a wire coathanger or more yarn to hang the cage from the ceiling. This can be done for any size animal, and the boxes can be painted or covered with paper if you so desire.

You will always have matching *wallpaper* for patching jobs if you hang a strip in the attic or closet where light and air will age it to match that which is on the wall!

Shelf paper secured with Scotch tape instead of thumb tacks is much less likely to tear, and will last a lot longer.

You can easily peel off old *contact paper* by placing a warm iron directly on the paper.

For a quick, inexpensive, and attractive way to line those closet shelves and kitchen cabinets, use *washable wallpaper*. Stores often sell rolls of discontinued patterns at discount prices. You will find these wallpapers are durable, especially the vinyls, and they are wider than the products usually made for shelving.

You can inexpensively glamorize your laundry area or any other room by using *travel posters* as "wallpaper." Apply with ordinary wallpaper paste, then spray with clear shellac to preserve them.

Putting new *wallpaper* over old? Cover the cracks with

masking tape. It won't show or crack through the new paper.

Covering the walls with *burlap* is marvelous for older homes with rough or cracked plaster walls. If you use a cellulose paste for the job, you will find it does not get lumpy, nor does it spoil. Mix the paste according to directions and apply to the wall instead of to the burlap. Be sure to measure and cut the burlap strips before the walls have been wet with paste.

If you prefer to work with wallpaper paste, apply plenty of it to the walls and the back of the burlap. Cut your burlap strips at least 3 inches longer than the wall to allow for shrinkage when they get wet. Start at the ceiling and smooth the burlap as you go down, butting the seams together as you would wallpaper. When it is dry, trim the burlap off next to the baseboard with a razor blade.

You will also find that there is an adhesive-backed burlap on the market now that comes in nine different colors.

What do you do with that leftover *paneling* after a project is done? There are so many uses for paneling that it should never be abandoned or pitched. Why not use the extra pieces to panel the walls of a closet? You might like to add a piece of cedar or pine in each closet to give a nice scent, although too much will cling to the clothes hanging there. If there isn't enough for a clothes closet, why not line your broom closet with it?

If you have paneled a room, did you cover the backs of the doors so that they blend in with the wall? This adds considerably to the over-all appearance of the room when the doors are closed.

Or, how about covering a desk, table, or bookcase in the paneled room to match? A knick-knack shelf or even a matching magazine rack can also be built from those left-over pieces of paneling.

Ever wish for a writing board that would reach from arm to arm on your favorite chair? One can be made from extra paneling. How about putting rubber suction cups on all four corners of the writing board so that you can read in the bathtub in comfort?

Other Redecorating Projects

Some bathrooms have a pedestal-type basin, and the sight of *exposed water pipes* can be a prime source of aggravation to the homemaker. The problem can be easily solved by purchasing an attractive fiber clothes hamper. Remove the top, cut out the back (half way down), and shove it back to the wall, enclosing the unsightly pipes. This decorative cover can be trimmed to match the existing shower and window curtain, and attractive decals can be added.

Would you like to cover those old-fashioned *radiators?* Housewives tell us about two different methods of doing so. They can be boxed in with veneer tops and louvered doors that can be opened to let the heat out into the room and closed when not in use. Stained in any color to match the decor of the room, the veneer tops will be handy for use as tables to hold flowers, centerpieces, ornaments, etc.

Or, make a wooden box frame surrounding the radiators. Then, take the slats from old venetian blinds and weave them in and out. Attach them to the frame, making an interesting-looking front for the radiator, yet providing enough ventilation for the heat to come through. They can be painted to match the room.

In almost all cases, you can save the price of new *stair treads* by removing the worn ones carefully, turning them over, and re-nailing.

If you have a dreary looking *window sill* that really

needs replacing, why not cover it with inexpensive mosaic tiles? The result will be not only very decorative, but simple to keep clean.

If you lack counter space in your kitchen, why not have a *cutting board* made of plywood to fit over the kitchen sink?

What can be done with those chains that hang from light fixtures in older homes, closets, utility rooms, etc.? Many a *pull chain* has been fashioned into an attractive mobile. If your imagination just doesn't seem to stretch in this direction, why not buy a mobile and pull the chain through the middle of it? You will find the mobile's movements are so intriguing that attention will be drawn away from an otherwise ugly chain.

Here is another idea for the home boasting hanging chains instead of wall switches. Purchase some gold chain at the hardware store and weave the pull chains through it. You can also purchase a gold hook to attach the chain to the ceiling, giving the appearance of an expensive swag fixture.

Or, purchase a lampshade which can be inverted to resemble a flowerpot. Place this over the light fixture, adding several strands of artificial ivy which have been fastened to the inside of the lampshade. You can then intertwine and cover the pull chain with the ivy, disguising it among the foliage of this "plant" which grows out of your ceiling.

You can add extra life to *window shades* which have become soiled or cracked by coating them with a rubber base house paint.

Would you like a fast and easy way to make your own decorative window shades? Upholstery vinyl—in any type of pattern—makes a lovely shade. Cut the vinyl to the correct length and width. Then, machine stitch a pocket for the wood slat, approximately 5 inches from the bottom of the shade. The lower edge can then be scalloped and rows of decorative fringe can be sewn on by machine. Staple or tape the vinyl to your roller, insert the wooden slat, and attach a curtain pull to the enclosed slat. A wooden valance or one made of matching vinyl can cover the roller for a professional custom-made looking shade.

Here is an excellent and inexpensive way to make lovely *cafe curtains*. Take the pillowcases which now come in so many colors and prints, as well as in several different sizes, open the seams for extra fullness, and create your own cafe curtains. They are not only kind to your budget, but are easy to launder.

Planning to replace the *linoleum* in your kitchen or utility room? Linoleum which has puffed up in spots is the mark of the do-it-yourselfer, but it needn't happen to you. Professional linoleum installers tell us that linoleum should be cut about ½ inch away from the walls so that it can stretch when it heats to room temperature. If you use linoleum adhesive and a bubble forms, simply prick the bubble with a pin to release the air if you cannot work it out at the sides. Some installers prefer to leave the molding or shoe strip at the baseboard off for at least three weeks to allow for stretching. The excess can then be trimmed off around the edges, and the molding can be replaced when the linoleum surface is perfectly flat.

If you plan to refinish your kitchen linoleum with a plastic-base *linoleum varnish*, use a new powderpuff as a brush and watch how smoothly it will spread the varnish.

Have trouble removing indoor–outdoor *carpet tiles*? Saturate the tiles with hot (not boiling) water and they will be much easier to remove.

When you are on a dollar-saving drive, squelch your bargain-hunting instincts when diving into that great mound of terrycloth *bath towels* "on sale." Why? Have you ever emerged from the shower and tried to sop up the water with a sleazy towel? It's pretty awful—no matter how little the price of the towel. Assuage your penny-pinching tendencies by realizing that the expensive towel is really a bigger savings in the long run. It not only retains its good looks through many a laundering, but lasts longer and is a real joy to use. Here is a good test when buying bath towels. Hold them up to the light. If you can see through them— don't buy them. The thicker the towel, the better it is! And, do check for shrinkage, especially at the borders. Bath towels with puckered edges will irritate you until you will want to "pitch" them long before their useful days are over.

Remember, too, to rub a portion of the material between your fingers. If a fine white powder comes off on your hands, the towel is filled with sizing which will wash out at the first laundering session.

Here is another hint for buying bath towels. Always buy *two* washcloths to match each towel. You will find the colors in the washcloth fade and wear out twice as fast as those in the towels.

·14·

Travel Savers

WHETHER YOU travel by plane or by car, whether you stay in a hotel or at a campsite, this chapter will provide you with many helpful ideas.

Packing and Traveling Abroad

Never leave a piece of luggage *half empty*. Your clothes will get shuffled around in transit.

When traveling, save room by rolling up your *belts*. Put them inside your shoes.

Luggage tags are often lost when traveling. However, the tags will stay on your luggage if you attach them with the gadget made for your keys which requires that you force the key between the two sections of a split metal ring. Simply attach the luggage tag to the ring and attach that to the metal section of the handle on your luggage. There is no way the tag can fall off when the luggage is being tossed around at the airport.

When you are on a trip and want to bring home something *fragile*, blow up a plastic bag as you would a balloon and close it tightly with a rubber band. It shouldn't be completely inflated. Use the bag to wrap the fragile item in. If you pack it in your suitcase, cushion it between layers of clothing.

Your *medicine bottles* will not leak in the suitcase if the tops are dipped in melted paraffin.

Line your *cosmetic bag* with different sizes of plastic sandwich bags. Find the proper size bag to fit and use one for each item. In case of spilled face powder or other accident, you will need only to throw that one plastic bag away and replace it.

When packing for the family vacation, pack the most brightly colored *pajamas* your family own. Why? Because white or pale pastel sleepwear can become "invisible" when tossed on the white sheets of a hotel or motel bed and can easily be left behind.

There is no need to drag your *dog's bowl* along when traveling. Save all those foil pans that frozen pot pies come in, and tuck some of them under the front seat. When you stop to eat, Rover can also drink and eat, with no mess to clean up afterwards.

When your husband needs several *ties* packed in his luggage, use shirt cardboards to prevent them from wrinkling. Cut three slits in the cardboard and thread the doubled ties through the slits. With this reinforcement, the ties will pack easily without shifting in the suitcase.

An overnight bag is just the place to keep those *samples* that come your way through the mail or are left at the door. Place such things as talcum powder, face powder, toothpaste, cold cream, perfume, etc., in the bag and they will be right there when you need them to make a trip.

They are handier than the regular-size products and cut down on the danger of spilling and waste.

When traveling by plane, keep a few *wash-and-dry* cleansing papers in your purse. Often, cocktails and dinner are served shortly after takeoff, and it is difficult to get out to wash your hands before the meal once the trays have been affixed.

If you pack a *flashlight*, be sure to put a piece of tape over the switch. It will keep the light from being turned on in the suitcase.

If you are visiting abroad and want to send back pretty *postcards*, enclose them in envelopes and affix first class postage to facilitate faster delivery.

Those paper packets of *cold-water soap* are a great convenience when you are traveling, especially out of the country. You can wash out drip-dries, including underclothes and hose, and have them ready to wear the next day. They will dry much faster if you wrap them in a dry towel and step on it a few times to get out much of the water.

If you are traveling abroad, remember most of the hotels in Europe do not provide *washcloths*. Take along a supply of Handy Wipes. They take up little room, make soft washcloths, and dry quickly.

Two *wakeup calls* at any hotel are better than one—the first one could be overlooked or you could fall asleep again. The backup call could prevent you from missing a plane flight!

Before taking off on a trip, read your *insurance policies*. It is important to know what is covered—and what is not.

When traveling, always pack a few *snap-type clothes-pins*. They will transform any coathanger into a pants or skirt hanger in a jiffy.

Make sure that any *imported items* you have to assemble yourself have English instructions. If you can't assemble what you buy, it is no saving. Open the package before you pay for the item and check the instruction sheet. Check, too, that measurements are for American tools and not in the metric system, to which many American-made tools are not calibrated.

Exotic spices, herbs, and unusual condiments found in foreign countries are inexpensive, easily packed and meet customs regulations. They make fine *souvenir gifts* for friends back home because some are not available in the United States, and the attractive packaging adds considerable interest.

A deck of playing cards also makes a nice souvenir, especially when decorated with scenic illustrations of places visited. Cards are inexpensive, lightweight, unbreakable, and pose no customs problem. They come in such a variety that they should make a hit with all your card-playing friends back home.

When you return from a vacation with many rolls of *film* to be developed, why not take along some self-addressed labels? The girl at the camera store will be glad you did—and it will save the time you would have stood around waiting for your name and address to be marked on each envelope.

You can add months to your *camera film* by storing it in the refrigerator. On removal from the refrigerator, bring the film to room temperature before using.

Here is another little trick for those of you who are

camera fans. You can remove corrosion on those hard-to-reach *terminals* which secure the batteries of your flash camera using the eraser on a long pencil. This little cleaning job sometimes puts new life in those old batteries that you thought would have to be replaced.

Don't waste those *flash bulbs* when taking pictures. If your subject is more than 17 feet away, the experts tell us no flash will light it. Keep this in mind when you see the countless flashes wasted in auditoriums and stadiums when the subjects are 100 or more feet away. If in doubt, read the instructions that came with your camera.

Incidentally, your *camera* can be a time and money saver for both you and your insurance company. Making a complete inventory of your possessions is a must, in case of fire or theft, but presenting photographs of each important possession will hasten the adjustments.

Camping, Fishing, and Picnics

Check the *tire inflation* on your boat trailer or camper if it is going to be hibernating for the winter. The experts tell us that being parked for a long time in the garage can be just as hard on tires as hundreds of miles of highway travel. Deflating the tires to half the recommended road pressure and putting the vehicle up on blocks is suggested.

When you go on a fishing trip take along that *crock pot* or slow cooker. You can then put food in the crock and turn it on before you leave the cabin in the morning. When you get back after 8 hours of fishing, you will have a good, hot meal waiting without any fuss.

Coat *kitchen matches* with colorless nail polish to keep

them dry on fishing, camping, and other outdoor trips. They will light every time.

For fishermen who need to have their *fishing license* available, take an old ballpoint pen, remove the cartridge, roll up the license, and insert it in the pen, clipping it to your pocket. The license will always be handy and dry.

Here is a dandy use for *reflective tape*. Attach a strip to flashlights so that they can be found quickly at home, on a camping trip, or in the trunk of the car.

Sew a pocket in each corner of the *tablecloth* you use for picnics. Then, place a stone in each pocket to prevent the wind from blowing the cloth off.

That cardboard *six-pack carton* can be a very handy gadget at the beach. It will hold your sunglasses, suntan lotion, wallet, watch, and even a paperback, a can of some beverage, or a candy bar. The carton protects these items from the sand and makes them easily accessible.

Your Car

Now that studded snow tires are illegal in many states, keep a bag of *rock salt* and a bag of coarse *sand* in your car trunk. Should you lose traction on an icy road, a shovel or two of sand will help. The salt, of course, will melt the snow.

A bag of *kitty litter* in the trunk of your car will also do a good job of getting you over the icy spots. Just a few handfuls under the rear wheels when you need traction on ice will do the trick.

Save gasoline. Cut your engine when your car will stand for more than one minute. Starting up again uses less gas than idling the engine for one minute.

Did you know that slightly loose *tire chains* give better traction and are less wearing on your tires?

When your car gets stuck in the snow and there is no sand or shovel available, remove the *rubber mats* from your car floor and place them in front of the rear wheels. This will probably give you enough traction to pull out.

When you don't have a set of chains to take along on that mountain trip, a few asphalt *roofing shingles* will do an admirable job. Place them under the spinning rear wheels and you will find that they give enough traction to pull the stalled auto right out. (The shingles should be placed with the gravel side down so that the rough surface can dig into the snow.) Do be sure to remove any nails from the shingles.

Try using a plastic *dustpan* to shovel snow from the car. It removes much more snow in less time than the snow brushes, and it won't mar your paint job.

Or, keep an old, soft *broom* handy in the car when traveling anywhere in snow country during the winter months. The broom is the quickest way to clean snow off the car.

When purchasing *jumper cables* for your car, buy copper rather than alumimum. They cost a little more, but they are well worth it. Remember, too, to keep a full tank of gas in cold weather. Gasoline can freeze when you have half a tank or less.

If your *car windows* frost up and you don't happen to have a snow and ice scraper handy, use your plastic credit card to clean off the windows. It won't hurt the card or scratch the windows, but it will remove Jack Frost's handiwork in a few moments.

A clean blackboard eraser is much handier than a

bulky cloth for wiping steam from your car windows. When not in use, it can be stored in the glove compartment.

No need to buy expensive *rust remover* for the chrome on your car. Just roll up a ball of aluminum foil, dampen it with water, and rub on the area. The rust spots will disappear.

Don't throw away that old zip-in *coat liner*. Store it in the trunk of your car. If your car breaks down, it will give you additional warmth and protect your clothing while you work on the car.

Wax that snow shovel. You will find the going a lot easier and the snow will not stick to the shovel.

Never *park* under trees or near electrical wires during a storm. Pull off the road where there are buildings and shelter.

For *tar* on automobiles, spray with laundry prewash. The tar will drip off with no damage to the finish of the car.

When you are traveling by car, snap the *map* you are using to the visor with a snap clothespin. It's much handier than having to forage through the glove compartment for the map.

To remove *spots and stains* from plastic car upholstery, wipe it with a solution of ¼ tablespoon of washing soda to 1 quart of warm water.

If you are a nonsmoker who becomes annoyed when people *smoke* in your car—why not fill the front ashtray with change for the toll road and the other ashtrays with wrapped hard candies?

Keep a roll of *paper towels* in your car. There are

dozens of uses for them: a lap napkin when eating in the car, a shoe cleaner, or a window cleaner.

Keeping the *children* amused while on a trip can be a problem—but it needn't be. There are two games on the market now that really do the job. One is "Auto Bingo" by Regal Manufacturing. It provides cards with pictured squares of familiar objects (flagpoles, schoolhouses, silos, etc.). The squares are covered as each object is sighted. The other popular game is Master-Mind by Invecta Manufacturing. It's a pegboard game that keeps little ones busy. Both games are available at toy stores for less than $5 each.

· 15 ·

Cleaning–Energy and Dollar Savers

HERE IS a chapter full of tips on how to cut down on your cleaning time—and money. Whether scrubbing your kitchen, your floors, or your furniture, you are sure to find them helpful.

Kitchen Cleaning

Having trouble keeping that *teapot* sweet and clean? There are several accepted methods for combating those stains. Sprinkle salt into the pot, rub well all around with a damp cloth, then rinse with boiling water. Or, fill the teapot with warm water and add 1 tablespoon of baking soda. Let it set a few minutes, then clean with a bottle brush.

Clean *copper* utensils by mixing a cup of flour and a teaspoon of salt with some vinegar. Rub the paste over the copper with a soft cloth, then polish with a bit of flannel chamois.

A mixture of salt and lemon juice makes a fine, inexpensive *brass cleaner*.

If you have *chrome* plates on your stove, try using cream silver polish on them. The grease will dissolve quickly, restoring the chrome to its original shine.

After frying *fish*, get rid of the odor in the pan by pouring in 2 tablespoons of vinegar, then filling with warm water. Speeds up the dishwashing, too, by loosening food particles.

To remove *rust* from a knife blade, plunge the blade into an onion and leave it there for an hour or so. Then, before you remove it, work the blade back and forth in the onion a few times. Finish off by washing and polishing as usual.

If the *bone handles* on your knives get discolored, you can clean them with hydrogen peroxide.

As soon as the guests leave the dinner party, "pre-spot" any wine, gravy, soup, or berry spots on your *tablecloth*. Keep a small bottle of liquid detergent on hand for this purpose. While the cloth is still on the table, remove the spots with the detergent. You will not ruin the finish of the table if there is a wipable pad under the tablecloth. It is so much easier to find the spots when the tablecloth is still on the table.

The next time someone spills *fruit juice* or *wine* on your favorite tablecloth, don't go into a tizzy. Quickly cover the spill with salt, and later rinse in cool water.

When wax *candles* drip and stick to your tablecloth or carpeting, place ice cubes in a plastic bag and apply to the wax. You will soon be able to lift the wax from the material.

A quick and easy way to remove the *egg tarnish* from a silver fork is to stick the tines into your silver polish and allow it to stay there until you are ready to wash it.

To remove *odors* from jars and bottles, pour a solution of water and dry mustard in them and allow to stand for several hours.

Boiling *potatoes* with jackets on in an aluminum pan will usually turn the pan black. Put a few drops of lemon juice in the water and the pan will stay shiny.

Did you know that *grapefruit rinds* are good for removing stains on porcelain? Before throwing them away, rub the inside of the rind over your kitchen sink (if it is porcelain), to get rid of those after-breakfast stains.

To get *old wax* out of candle holders, put them in the freezer for awhile. The wax will loosen and drop right out.

You can easily light the candles in glass "hurricane" and other *deep candle holders* that are hard to reach with an ordinary match, by lighting a strand of regular spaghetti. The spaghetti doesn't break, and you will avoid singed fingers.

Candles will last a lot longer and burn without smoking or dripping if you coat them (all but the wicks) with *soapsuds*. Let them dry in the candleholders before lighting.

To easily clean an *eggbeater*, beat it in cool soapsuds. Heat will congeal the egg.

Here is an inexpensive *oven cleaner:* A pan of hot water and a tablespoon or two of ammonia left in a greasy oven overnight is as effective as the more expensive store-bought cleaners.

If your formerly bright *aluminum pans* are now dull,

they will soon shine again if you boil some apple peelings in them. Or, rub them with a cloth dipped in lemon juice.

Here is a prescription for dull, spotted *kitchen appliances*. Borrow your husband's favorite paste car wax and apply as directed. It cleans as well as polishes and a little buffing will restore the appliance to its original beauty. It also helps keep it that way longer!

If you own some good china with an *embossed design*, perhaps you are afraid of the border wearing off from being stacked with one plate or saucer on top of another. Buy a length of flannel and cut circles with pinking shears to fit between each of the stacked pieces. It will protect the design, making it look like new for many years to come.

Wrap the *silver* that isn't in constant use in tarnish-preventive flannel to cut down on polishing.

Never immerse a *vacuum bottle* in water to wash. Water may seep into the metal barrel. Clean the inside with detergent and water or with water and baking soda. Rinse thoroughly. Place upside down to dry. Leave uncapped to keep the bottle fresh.

If something cooks over in the *oven*, sprinkle salt on it at once and you will be able to lift the mess up as soon as the oven cools.

Spray foamy *bathroom cleaner* on the stove and refrigerator. You will find it cuts grease and dirt in a jiffy and leaves a nice fragrance and shine.

For sparkling kitchen *appliances*, dampen a cloth with a solution of half water and half ammonia, and dry with a clean cloth.

You can keep those electric *stove burners* clean while

you are cooking if you cover the unused ones with foil pie tins turned upside down. These are easily washed for use again.

All *can openers* need very careful cleaning of the cutting edge. If your can opener is electric, you cannot immerse the appliance in water, but you can clean the cutting blade. It is easily removed. Use hot, soapy water and a stiff small brush to get under the teeth of the blade.

Frying pans used for *fish* can be kept clean and odorless by sprinkling with salt before washing.

If you break an *egg* on the floor, sprinkle it heavily with salt, let stand for about 10 minutes, then just sweep it up into the dustpan.

Give your automatic *dishwasher* a vinegar treatment so that your holiday dishes and crystal will sparkle. Push the button for regular cycle (without soap). When the machine fills with water, open the door and add a cup of white vinegar. Allow the cycle to run. This will dissolve deposits in pipes and parts.

Lime deposits on your *tea kettle* can greatly shorten its life expectancy. To do away with these blights, add one part vinegar to three parts water and boil a few minutes. Let the pot stand overnight before cleaning it out, and your tea kettle will be fresh and clean again.

Stubborn stains on *nonstick cookware* can be removed by boiling 2 tablespoons of baking soda, ½ cup liquid household bleach, and 1 cup of water in the cookware for 10 minutes. Re-season the pan by rubbing well with salad oil.

When you open a box of *baking soda* to place in your refrigerator, mark the date on the box. Then change the box regularly so that the inside of your refrigerator will always smell sweet and clean.

Ever have a plastic *bread wrapper* melt onto your electric coffee maker or toaster? Dampen a cloth, and make a mild abrasive with baking soda. This will remove the plastic without scratching the surface of the appliance.

Try fastening sheets of *aluminum foil* to all four sides of your oven with small, all-metal magnets when roasting meats that tend to spatter. It will save hours of cleaning.

If you have a polished or brushed steel *sink*, try using silver cream to clean it instead of the usual harsh cleansers. It won't scratch the finish and will do as good a job.

Stubborn *tea stains* in a cup? They can be easily removed by rubbing with a bit of salt.

Once table *salt* has pitted your good silver shakers, the damage cannot be removed. Remember to remove the salt from silver shakers each time before you store them and avoid problems.

Windows and Doors

Ironing curtains, tablecloths, or other large pieces is easier if you turn the ironing board around so that you iron on the wide end and rest the iron on the narrow end.

When you line-dry a *chenille bedspread*, turn the tufts inside out and rub them together to make them fluffier as they dry.

When washing those *quilted mattress pads* use warm, not hot, water. Remove from the dryer when still slightly damp, and stretch and straighten them before putting on the line. Quilted articles sometimes tend to pucker and shrink.

To cover a window when you need to send your *draperies* to be cleaned, hang any fabric (even sheets) with those travel-type spring clothespins—the plastic ones with hooks. It takes only seconds to hook the clothespins over the drapery rod.

You can save dollars by *laundering* and line drying those draperies at home without having ugly clothespin marks or line marks on them if you put a few plastic or stainless steel drapery hooks back into the headings just before hanging them on the line. You can then hook the draperies over the clothesline.

One-half cup of any brand of car *windshield washer solvent* in a gallon of water will wash and shine windows, mirrors, chrome, etc., without any streaks.

A small *bottle-washing brush* is handy for removing dust from corners of the windowpane molding when you wash your windows.

Spread those *washable window shades* on the kitchen floor. Use a sponge and warm sudsy water. Overlap strokes, and rinse with clear water for a fast, easy, and effective job.

Here is an easy make-it-yourself *window cleaner* that can be put into a spray bottle. Eight parts of water to one part vinegar constitutes the simple solution. It does a good job on mirrors, too.

Louvered doors can always be a problem to clean. Why not take a new 2-inch paint brush and a pan of household cleaner, and clean away. Dip the brush into the cleaner and "paint" the doors. Rinse, and you will find beautifully clean doors easily done in a very short time.

To avoid *streaked* windows, don't wash them on a sunny day.

For streakless window panes (on the inside) wait until dark to wash them. Every little streak and smudge you might miss will show up at night.

Wash glass doors and windows with vertical strokes on one side and horizontal strokes on the other, so that if there are streaks you can tell in a jiffy which side they are on.

The popular *window blinds* can pose a real housekeeping problem unless you use Endust on your cloth. Spray it on the cloth, close the blinds, and clean one side. Reverse the blinds and repeat on the other side.

One-half cup of *cornstarch* in a gallon of warm water will not only make your windows sparkle, but will also clean your refrigerator and other appliances easily.

Rugs and Floors

For best results, do not *shampoo* your rugs on days when the humidity is high, but wait for a sunny, dry day.

When a *grease spot* appears on carpeting it can grow bigger and bigger if you don't catch it as soon as possible. Just brush baking soda into the stain and let it set overnight. The next morning, vacuum up the soda and the stain.

Ever try removing a spot on the carpeting with foamy shaving cream? It is ready for instant use and is often more effective and drier than the foam you whip up from powdered or liquid detergents.

When a *contact lens* is lost in the shaggy carpet, place a piece of nylon hose over the nozzle of a vacuum attachment and go over the area. This should pick up the lens. This is also effective when the lens has been lost in the grass outdoors.

Ever try removing *soot* from carpeting by sprinkling salt over the soiled area? Wait a half hour, then vacuum up the salt and the soot will come with it.

Quick action with an ice cube will remove *coffee and cola stains* from carpeting. Blot the spill immediately with a terrycloth towel. Rub the ice cube briskly over the spot.

Keep small bottles of *carbonated soda water* on hand during the holidays as a super cleaner when spills occur. Blot the spill quickly with a towel, then apply the soda with a clean cloth, rubbing as briskly as the fabric will allow.

Do you like to buy your *floor wax* in the large, economy size can? If so, you might find it very hard to work with. Why not pour the wax into an empty plastic bottle—the kind which once held liquid detergent? It will be much easier to work with, and you can squirt out just the amount you need without danger of waste.

When you wax the kitchen floor, wash and wax the tips of the kitchen *chair legs* as well. This will prevent scratch marks on the floor.

Have the children crushed *crayon* into your carpeting? Moisten the spot and rub in full-strength liquid or dry detergent. It may be necessary to repeat the process several times. If the color remains, use oxygen bleach and rinse well.

After *shampooing* a carpet, put the furniture back in place with its legs in the individual cups of cardboard egg cartons. Just separate the cups of the cartons with sharp scissors. There will be no danger of rust stains.

To easily remove wax from the felt pads on your *floor polisher*, place felt pads between several thicknesses of newspaper and press with a warm iron. The newspaper will absorb the wax. Repeat if necessary.

To make sure that most of the floor wax you use goes on the floor and not in the *applier pad*, soak the pad in cold water before using. You will use less energy and less wax with this method!

If you don't own an electric *floor polisher*, rent one for the big pre-holiday shine up. Do not press down on the handle of the polisher when operating it. For best results, allow the wax to dry at least 30 minutes before using the polisher. To save money, clean the floors and put the wax on them before picking up your rented polisher.

Clay *kitty litter* does a great job of absorbing oil spots on the garage floor.

Painting the *basement floor* will be a lot easier if you apply the paint with a roller which has been fastened securely to a mop handle. You will be able to stand upright while doing the job.

When grease or oil is spilled on *indoor–outdoor carpeting*, spray the spots with a prewash spray and let it sit several minutes. Then take the hose and rinse it, and watch the spots disappear.

To remove *acid spots* on an oak floor, rub with a cloth treated with liquid paste wax.

Put a few dried beans in the disposable *vacuum cleaner bag*. The air agitates them, compacting the dust, making bag changes less frequent.

Too much *shampoo* solution will not make your rugs cleaner. The action of the brush does the cleaning. Use the shampoo sparingly and rinse well.

Furniture

White circles on furniture caused by wet glasses can usually be removed if you apply camphorated oil with a piece of cotton. Allow it to remain overnight, then polish with furniture polish.

Stale beer does a splendid job of cleaning leather-covered furniture. Or, rub the leather with half a lemon and then shine with a dry cloth.

Airplane glue or cement on furniture will usually yield when rubbed over with cold cream.

The plastic *patio furniture* has a tendency to gather dust and dirt more readily than wood. Silicone cleaners will miniminze the buildup. However, this furniture does need a good washing on occasion. Use a solution of water and your dishwashing detergent. Do not use abrasives. (Toothpaste, which is a very mild abrasive, can be used on minor scratches if you test it first on an inconspicuous spot.)

You can remove *candle wax* from wooden furniture with a hand dryer held slightly above the drips to soften the wax. It is then easily removed with a paper towel, with no scratches!

When moving *mattresses*, cover them with two fitted sheets. It is a lot easier to wash the sheets than to try and spot-clean the mattresses.

Dusting and Polishing

A *child's dust mop* is the perfect tool to reach into those places that are hard to dust. Its swivel head will hug the top of door jambs, etc.

Here is a solution you can make yourself for cleaning your *walls*. Combine 2 ounces of pure borax, 1 teaspoon of ammonia, and 2 quarts of water. Apply this solution with a soft cloth—and you will need no soap. There will be a minimum of streaking, as this solution really does a good job.

Remember to dust those walls before washing them, and always wash from the bottom up (to prevent streaks from running down into soiled sections).

Remove the shades and bulbs before washing or polishing your *lamps*. Washable shades can be cleaned with a mild detergent and warm water, and suspended on a line to dry. Be sure the trim is sewn, not glued, before washing.

Did you know that if your *lamp bulbs* are dusty, you aren't using a good deal of the electric light you are paying for?

Use those large brown *grocery bags* to clean the dust from a dry mop. Just insert the mop head into the bag, hold the bag closed at the top, and move the handle up and down. The dust falls right into the bag for easy disposal.

A paper plate cut in half makes a fine emergency *dustpan*.

You can make your own good, inexpensive dusting and *polishing cloth* by taking a soft, absorbent old piece of material, sprinkling it lightly with water and then with furniture polish. Roll the whole thing up into a ball and let it stand for ten minutes. Your homemade dusting cloth will do a good job of removing finger marks as well as the dust.

Wiping *chrome* legs of kitchen chairs with a cloth moistened with furniture polish removes light dirt and helps make them easy to keep clean.

How do you clean *oil paintings?* The experts say we should do nothing more than dust them. Superficial dust and dirt can be removed by a light brushing with absorbent cotton or a soft brush. (A discarded shaving brush is ideal.) Do *not* use soap, water, erasers, raw potatoes, or raw onions, as may be suggested by well-meaning friends. If the painting needs restoring or a thorough cleaning, take it to an expert.

After washing and drying an *oiled mop*, add a few drops of oil polish to the strings and store in a closed metal can. Oiled mops can ignite spontaneously if not kept in this manner.

Hang a small *whisk broom* on a hook attached to your upright vacuum cleaner. It will be very handy to brush out the corners that the vacuum cannot get into.

That pretty *feather duster* is back in business. It is about the only contraption that successfully dusts the new thin metal venetian blinds.

Parchment lampshades should be conditioned periodically with castor oil. Clean imitation parchment shades with liquid wax.

Spray *plastic flowers* with hair spray to keep them from looking dusty.

Easily and quickly clean your favorite *plants* by donning a pair of cotton work gloves. Lightly wet the fingers and dust quickly and gently.

Keep an old *paint brush* in your cleaning supply kit. It is handy for dusting delicate things like picture frames, hand-carved furniture, and light bulbs.

Try your *silver cream* as a cleaner for light switches, plastic wastebaskets, and even that plastic clothes hamper!

A *pipe cleaner* will do a good job of cleaning those intricate parts of your record player or sewing machine.

You can easily and quickly de-rust and polish the metal parts of your *golf clubs* by using a jeweler's rouge cloth.

Varnish stains can be removed from fabrics by saturating with turpentine or mineral spirits, rubbing between the hands, and then sponging with alcohol.

Plastic bowl and appliance covers, even plastic curtains, can remain soft and pliable and last very much longer if two or three drops of mineral oil are added to the final rinse water when these items come up for washing.

What is the easiest way to get *crayon marks* off the wall? Paste wax will do the trick if the walls are enameled. Soap and water with a bit of borax will remove the marks from other washable walls. If your little artist has chosen wallpaper surface for his creative efforts, sponge the marks lightly with a soft cloth dipped in cleaning fluid. Washable papers may be given a final soap-and-water treatment. If the cleaning fluid leaves a definite ring on non-washable paper, try a poultice of fuller's earth and water.

Crayon marks on your kitchen tiles? Try a dab of silver polish as a quick remover.

Did you know a lump of *alum* placed in your silver drawer will keep your silver from tarnishing?

The next time you launder your *shower curtains*, spray them with a stain remover, especially around the bottom, running them through the warm water cycle with terry towels as scrubbers. Hang them to dry and they will be good as new!

Old stains or *rust* on utility room tubs can be easily soaked away with vinegar or lemon juice.

You can easily freshen your *bed pillows* by tossing them into the dryer with a fabric softener sheet for 15 minutes. However, *don't* put foam pillows in the dryer.

Removing the smoke from your *fireplace stone* can be your easiest cleaning chore. Make tracks to an art supply store and buy an art-gum eraser. Start erasing. You will find this works especially well on porous, rock-front fireplaces.

A bucket of cold water poured quickly into the *bathroom bowl* will carry most of the standing water out, making it much easier to scrub. This also saves on cleanser, as it is not lost in all that standing water. Flush to rinse.

To remove brown stains from *vases*, put a few pieces of finely chopped raw potatoes in the vase. Add a half cup of vinegar and shake. Wash with warm, soapy water. Rinse well and dry.

For hard-to-clean *brass* such as door plates, use a mixture of salt and lemon juice.

One of the best cleansers for *pewter* is a homemade mixture of wood ashes moistened with water. Simply rub it on your pewter piece. Not only will it clean, but it also helps retain the desired dull sheen.

Have trouble cleaning the back walls and corners of deep *cabinets*? Try using a long-handled tub-cleaning sponge mop. You can sit or kneel on the floor and scrub away.

A large *brown paper bag* can save many steps for you as you do your household chores. Attach a pants hanger to one side of it so you can hang it on the doorknob of each room. Use it for emptying ashtrays, wastebaskets, and other debris you gather as you clean.

• • •

Someday perhaps a neighbor will look at *you* with envy. Maybe you will have just bought a new car or mink jacket, or taken a delightful trip. Silently, they might wonder how you did it. (Do you have a rich uncle? Have you been feeding those kids beans every day?) The answer will be very simple . . . you have learned to be a wise and thrifty homemaker!

Index